Int|AR

Interventions | **Adaptive Reuse**

Editors In Chief:
Markus Berger
Liliane Wong

Special Editor:
Damian White

Graphic Design Editor:
Ernesto Aparicio

Int|AR is an annual publication by the editors in chief: Markus Berger + Liliane Wong,
and the Department of Interior Architecture, Rhode Island School of Design.

Members of the Advisory Board:
- Heinrich Hermann, Chair of Architecture & Design, Alfred State; Head of the Advisory Board, Co-Founder of Int|AR
- Uta Hassler, Chair of Historic Building Research and Conservation, ETH Zurich.
- Brian Kernaghan, Professor Emeritus of Interior Architecture, RISD.
- Niklaus Kohler, Professor Emeritus, Karlsruhe Institute of Technology.
- Dietrich Neumann, Royce Family Professor for the History of Modern Architecture and Urban Studies at Brown University;
  President, Society of Architectural Historians.
- Theodore H M Prudon, Professor of Historic Preservation, Columbia University; President of Docomomo USA.
- August Sarnitz, Professor of History of Architecture, Academy of Fine Arts Vienna.
- Friedrich St Florian, FAIA, Professor of Architecture Emeritus, RISD; Principal, Friedrich St. Florian Architects, Providence, RI.
- Wilfried Wang, O'Neil Ford Centennial Professor in Architecture, University of Texas, Austin; Hoidn Wang Partner, Berlin.

Layout_ Yoon Kim, Khanh Luu

Design coordination_Yoon Kim

Intar Student team_ Cathy Ha, Sarah Burgett-Leutner, Lindsay Winstead

Copy Editor_ Pamela Harrington

Cover Design_Ernesto Aparicio, Khanh Luu

Cover Photo_ courtesy Lore Mellemans

Inner Cover Photos_ Clara Halston

Printed by SYL, Barcelona

Distributed by Birkhäuser Verlag GmbH, Basel P.O. Box 44, 4009 Basel, Switzerland, Part of De Gruyter

Int|AR Journal welcomes responses to articles in this issue and submissions of essays or projects for
publication in future issues. All submitted materials are subject to editorial review. Please address feedback,
inquiries, and other material to the Editors, Int|AR Journal, Department of Interior Architecture,
Rhode Island School of Design, Two College Street, Providence, RI 02903 www.intar-journal.edu,
email: INTARjournal@risd.edu

CONTENTS

CRITICAL RESILIENCE
CRITICAL RECONSTRUCTION

SPECIAL EDITOR Damian White with Markus Berger & Liliane Wong

Stephen Jay Gould once pithily observed that "nature does not exist for us, had no idea we were coming, and doesn't give a damn about us.[1] " The ever more disturbing news that emerges from the most recent report of the Intergovernmental Panel on Climate Change[2], would seem to suggest that "nature in the large" can accommodate to a world warmed by greenhouse gases. Whether this will be a world that provides optimal conditions for human flourishing, is, a matter that is considerably less certain. In this issue of INTAR, we attempt to grapple with the extent to which design strategies – moving from the local to the global, the discrete to the overarching - might allow us to envisage more resilient worlds. Gould would no doubt have approved of interior architecture and adaptive reuse turning to ecology to understand, anticipate and find humane and creative ways to adapt to future impacts. Nevertheless, his writings and essays also persistently warn that given the dark legacies of Malthusianism and social Darwinism, we have to acknowledge that ecological metaphors and concepts have to be handled with care. This is because scientific concepts and metaphors transported into domains beyond their original intention, can end up as power forces that order our age and not always for the better.

The central concept informing this issue on "resilience" emerges out of scientific ecology, one that can be traced to the writings of the ecologist C.S. Hollings (1973)[3]. It denotes a shift in ecology from an older focus on the balance of nature and equilibrium relationships, to the view that ecosystems are actually characterized by multiple stable states, tipping points, non-linear processes and non-equilibrium relations. Hollings maintained that adaptive management of the structure and functions of ecosystems may well require attending to the capacity of ecosystems to absorb change without flipping into a new state of being. Hollings' research pre-dates contemporary concerns with global climate change. His deployment of the concept of resilience as a defining feature of the age has subsequently taken on quite a remarkable life of its own.

Popularized in part by the prominent role of *The Stockholm Resilience Institute* and their discussions of "planetary boundaries"[4], concerns about resilience have quickly moved beyond the environmental sciences. Increasingly, resilience is understood today as "the ability of a system to absorb change whilst retaining essential function; to have the ability for self organization; and to have the capacity to adapt and learn.[5]" It is the very plasticity of this definition of resilience that has seen the concept move through the social sciences to enter discussions in public policy, defense and security conversations, issues surrounding humanitarian aid, international relations and even welfare.

Critics, ever attuned to the entanglement between science and society, have observed that it is the ubiquity of the concept that should trigger alarm bells. Mark Neocleous for example[6] has observed that the very popularity of resilience for policy makers involved in imposing austerity budgets on their populations should make us wary. Neocleous argues that for those isolated and left behind as welfare states crumble, the central mantra of the age has become "buck up and be resilient!". From this perspective then, the growth of the concept of resilience tracks rather too closely, the continued globalization of neo-liberal ideas, western militarism and the making of neo-liberal subjects.

That the concept of resilience can be used by various actors in problematic ways cannot be denied. Yet, in this respect, it is no different than "conservation", "sustainable development", "mutualism", "self reliance", "socialism", "communism", the list could go on endlessly. All have meant one thing at one point in time and re-appropriated for other uses in other contexts. The meaning of terms and the use of concepts though are not static or fixed but fluid and subject to different kinds of appropriations by different kinds of forces. The critical question is rather whether resilience can be conceptualized, understood and deployed in different ways?

This issue of INTAR suggests that from the perspective of design, resilience has to be a central concern of the future of material making but it can also open up more creative ways of thinking about world making. Design has to attend to resilience and adaptability, since resilience and adaptability at a very elementary level are critical aspects of how our built environments

relate to and react to change. The Department of Interior Architecture at RISD is persistently grappling with the active and passive approaches of change. Change will happen, either without human intervention, where material decay and the resilience of nature takes back its own, or as a set of human interventions driven by need, desire or hope to create resilience in structures, systems and the environment.

Moreover, lack of attention to the relations between social, ecological, and infrastructural resilience can further contribute to all manner of further injustices. As we have seen from Hurricane Katrina, a disregard for the resilience of basic infrastructure can lead to disaster, disaster born by some groups rather than others. Indeed, it could be suggested that few gestures will create more human suffering in the years ahead than a failure to attend to how our built environment will have to be rendered more resilient in the face of climate change. As Hanna observes, (2011:219)[7] in a warming world, it is the socially isolated and immobile old people, the sick, young children from lower income families, those who cannot afford air conditioning, those affected by poor quality housing stock and those who work outside and are remunerated by output that are all much more vulnerable to chronic heat exposure and even death than the affluent. Neo-liberal conceptualizations of re-silience have to be guarded against but there are other ways of engaging with this concept and other conversa-tions to be had.

Through the ideas of our authors in this issue, it can be seen that careful and thoughtful attention to the con-cept of resilience in the (re)design of the built environ-ment can open up a very broad range of creative strate-gies for adaptive reuse. Our first article aptly states that in design at least, the field is "wide open." In this volume, the exuberance and diversity of ways in which this con-cept has facilitated new design strategies for the built environment suggests that we need to be cautious of discussing resilience in one dimensional ways.

And in the end our investigation of resilience re-vealed as much about ourselves as about applications of terminology. Our interview with Sicilian architect Roberto Collovà, yielded an unexpected revelation. As

he discusses the history of Sicily and the resilience of the Sicilian peoples to domination, both historic and modern, a different resilience emerges, notably; a body of architectural work that spans more than three de-cades and is the result of a resilient spirit, dedicated to a belief in an eternal architecture that has, in present day, been submerged in an all too rapidly changing digital landscape. Derived from disaster recovery, Professor Collovà's work resolves itself in painstaking resolution of pure architectural ideal, expressed in built, written and photographed form. With a sole reliance on principle, he negotiates the world with infinite patience and ethical dedication. His work and the work of all the contributors to this edition suggests the debate about resilience, who owns the concept and how the concept is deployed, is no simple matter.

Providence 2014

ENDNOTES

1 Stephen Jay Gould, "The Golden Rule - A Proper Scale for Our Environmental Crisis," Natural History 99 (Sept. 1990.)

2 Working Group I Contribution to the IPCC Fifth Assessment Re-port Climate Change 2013: The Physical Science Basis Summary for Policymakers.

3 C.S. Hollings "Resilience and stability of ecological systems" in: Annual Review of Ecology and Systematics. Vol 4 :1-23.

4 Anderies JM, Carpenter SR, Steffen W, Rockstrom J (2012) "The Topology of Non-Linear Global Carbon Dynamics: From Tipping Points to Planetary Boundaries" Center for the Study of Institu-tional Diversity, Working Paper Series #CSID-2012-009.

5 W. Neil Adger, Katrina Brown, and James Waters "Resilience" in John Dryzek, Richard Norgaard, David Schlosberg (ed.), The Oxford Handbook of Climate Change and Society. London OUP Press, 2011:696.

6 Mark Neocleous "Resisting Resilience" Radical Philosophy 178 (Mar/Apr 2013)

7 Elizabeth Hanna (2011), 'Health Hazards', in John Dryzek, Richard Norgaard, David Schlosberg (ed.), The Oxford Handbook of Climate Change and Society, Oxford, OUP Press.

LEFT
Roberto Collovà in his studio, Palermo, Italy

RIGHT
Case di Stefano, Gibellina

WIDE OPEN

ON CHANGE AND ADAPTATION OF BUILT FORMS

by MARCO VANUCCI

The ability to change and adapt is a necessary condition for the successful fit of an organism within its environment.

This should be true not only within nature but also within the built scape. To remain current and 'future-proof' architecture requires the ability to constantly morph itself according to the current socio-economic and natural context.

Architecture though is still very much conceived and treated as a static, lifeless entity. This vision of architecture, aligned to the utilitarian paradigm "form follows function," reflects a static and outdated vision of society. The mutable nature of contemporary society reveals the drawback of a functional approach to architectural forms.

Architecture should instead be conceived as a living organism whose survival in a hostile environment depends on its ability to change and adapt within the context of conservative use of resources.[1] Thus the development of adaptive architecture contemplates an integral relationship with the surrounding eco-system where an economical use of energy and matter is the necessary prerequisite for a resilient new built environment.

The ever-changing contemporary urban and sub-urban conditions require a more sustainable and dynamic model: the fast turning economic instability has revealed the shortcomings of the contemporary built environment, designed and built to last but not to adapt. Modern architecture attempted to address change by developing 'generic' buildings within rigidly 'zoned' planning strategies. In the Modernist project, the generic provides the desirable degrees of flexibility in the equation form-function: the open grid is employed as an undifferentiated organizational matrix; the open plan provides homogeneous spatial qualities. This model proved its dramatic shortcomings when faced with the new needs of a changing world order.

The radical avant-garde of the 60's and 70's explored extensively the notion of a more nomadic, flexible urban condition. These were seductive visions of a glamorous future of the Machine Age, leaving however both social and environmental issues unaddressed.

Many years later, the questions posed by the late XX Century avant-garde are still relevant and open to multiple radical interpretations. How can architectural design address the need for a more adapting built environment while retaining necessary social functionality as well

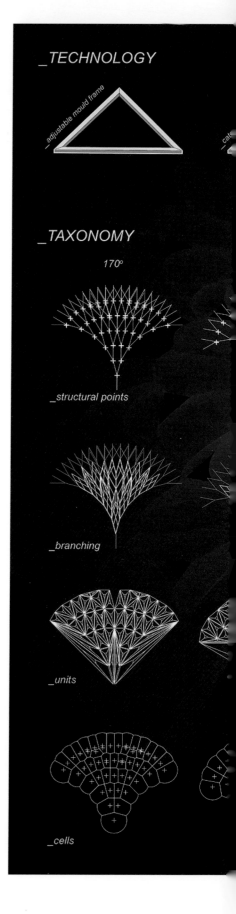

_TECHNOLOGY

_adjustable mould frame

_TAXONOMY

170°

_structural points

_branching

_units

_cells

_elastic cloth

_casting FRP

_monocoque shell

_glazing

160°   155°   150°   145°

as qualitative relevance? In other words, how can we design our buildings and cities in a context where change and uncertainty seem to be the only sure thing?

Today more than ever, in a context of rapid transformation and global challenges (economic, social and environmental), the role of the avant-garde seems even more pressing than in the past: the search for innovation, in fact, represents not just a vital form of speculation and critique; it becomes an imperative character of the fittest to survive the contemporary social, economic, technological and environmental challenges. How does architectural design seek relevant innovation and novelty?

Evolutionary biology offers an interesting perspective on the unpredictable nature of the future and change. In nature, evolution and adaptation occur through the specialized use of biomechanical characteristics; those employed for tasks different from the ones for which it was initially utilized.[2] In other words, it is through the specialization of (initially) marginal tasks that living forms evolve and adapt to unpredictable future circumstances. Our hands, for instance, have the same characteristics as the hands of the primates: their capacity of playing musical instruments is a functional adaptation initiated as a specialized path. Thus, evolution occurs via the latent capacity of living forms to specialize tasks and adapt to unforeseen needs.

In this case the randomized nature of evolution and specialization is what defines the capacity for living forms to adapt. The human eye, for instance, probably descends from light-sensitive cells. These photo-receptive tissues have transformed along an extended and non-oriented path: initially driven by chance and then regulated by natural selection.

The casual specialization of tasks towards the not-yet-defined needs or functional purposes is what guides the evolutionary process and allows the fittest to adapt to the changing environment. In nature, adaptation is addressed through the redundant capacity of living systems to perform multiple tasks within an economic use of their resources: nature does more with less. A spider, for instance, uses its silk web to create its habitat and perform a multiplicity of different tasks. The spider eats, moves, sleeps, and constructs its living space with the same material using the same construction process.

In this sense, the impossibility to predict the future scenario is addressed by the redundant production of multi-directional specialized solutions. Moving away from the idea of innovation as a (sophisticated) response to a specific need/scenario opens the way to a new understanding of sustainable design.

A novel architectural sensitivity is arising out of the current crisis: one that sees the biological paradigm as the starting point for new architectural experimentation. Leaving aside the ideological approach to the idea of progress, contemporary avant-garde architecture is

turning towards an opportunistic pragmatism that is replacing the dogmatic idealism of the late XX Century. The homogeneous matrix of Modernism is replaced by heterogeneous spatial qualities. Differentiation replaces uniform standardization. A new sensitivity toward a performance-base architecture is blossoming: form follows performance.

In this context, technology plays a paramount role in shaping the horizon of possibility. Advances in material science and construction processes are among the most impactful undertakings of the new century. Many are already predicting the advent of self-constructing, moving architecture built out of organic, self-healing matter. We can't certainly predict what the future will be like. What's certain is that tomorrow's ideas are already circulating and will soon turn into built form.

The paradigmatic shift introduced by novel fabrication processes - from file to fabrication-, together with the innovation in material sciences and computational

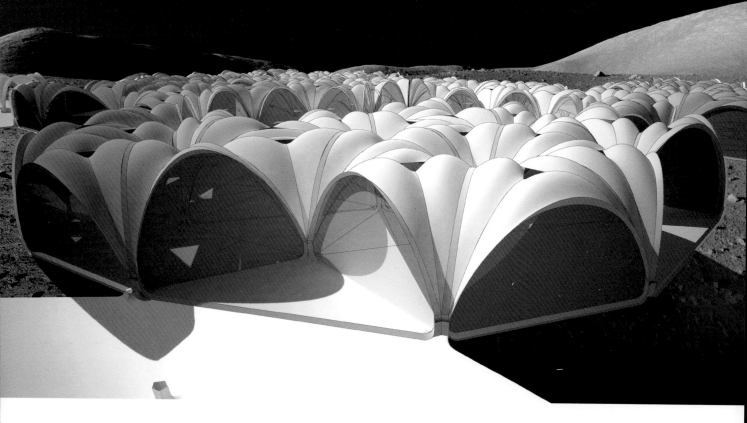

technologies - from product to process- allowed the introduction of a novel approach towards architecture and its relationship with the environment: from context neutral to context-aware design.

The systemic integration of architecture with the environment and within its constituent parts is one essential feature of the new architectural paradigm. Architecture as a system has a twofold characteristic: systems as whole and generating systems.[3] The former is concerned with the holistic property which can only be understood as a product of interaction among parts. The latter – generating system- is a kit of parts, with rules about the way these parts may be combined.

Every "system as a whole" is generated by a generating system.

"To ensure the holistic system property of buildings and cities we must invent generating systems, whose parts and rules will create the necessary holistic system properties of their own accord". (C. Alexander)[4]

Finally, a new kind of architecture is emerging: one that privileges the ephemeral over the static; the temporary over the firm; the contextual over the generic; the hybrid over the homogeneous; the informal over the rigid. The field is wide open.

ENDNOTES

1 Pierce, Introduction - structure in nature, in *Structure in Nature is a strategy for design*. Edited by MIT Press (1990), xiii.

2 Filippo Innocenti, "Past Shock", City Vision Magazine (2012) : http://pastshock.wordpress.com/2012/12/07/161/

3 C. Alexander, "Systems generating systems", in *Computational Design Strategies*. Edited by Achim Menges and Sean Ahlquist (Wiley AD 2011), p58.

4 Ibidem

THE URBAN BACKDOOR
REPLACING THE MEDIATOR IN ARCHITECTURAL PUBLIC SPACE

by FABRIZIO GESUELLI + CHIARA ANDREOTTI

A mediator is a medium that operates in a "space of transformation"[1] by interposing itself between two poles. What does the denial of mediation signify in an architectural framework? This is the question that this paper will address by exploring the meaning of protest, an action that provides the capacity for denying mediation. Protest goes straight to the target. It thrives on the claim that it is anti-hierarchical.

Before proceeding with the analysis of protest and how it affects mediation and hierarchies, it is useful to introduce two concepts: first, how mediation is intended in architecture; second, the nature of the figure of mediator.

Mediation, in an architectural framework, stands for an implicit or explicit set of rules or, quoting Marc Augé, "instructions for use"[2] that must be followed by users when using a space. An example of mediation is found in airports, for instance, when individuals are waiting for a flight in the lounge of an airport and read the signal "no smoking". That signal instructs on the use of that space. Mediation thus generates a hierarchical relationship between users and spaces, notably imposing on the former the rules for using the latter (if I wanted to smoke I should rather find a smoking space inside the airport).[3]

The previous example also introduces the second concept of mediation, one that provides the capacity for establishing relationships between terms belonging to different systems. The nature of these relationships is exactly the object of debate in this article.

In the airport there are two systems, no smoking and smoking areas, with individuals that oscillate between them. Individuals, although they are in between, are not mediators. Rather the mediator is the airport, globally intended as a space that hosts both smoking and no smoking areas. The airport acts as a street-sweeper,[4] which creates order, chasing out disorder. Ultimately, the airport is a space with a series of hierarchical instructions that mediate with users. These instructions establish relationships which are not mutual but where one factor has priority over another.

One could argue, how does the protest fit with all this? The answer to the question must be addressed in terms of hierarchy and how protest tends to deny it.

Last Judgement: hierarchy and protest
Michelangelo's *Last Judgement* in its representation of a biblical story can be viewed as an act of protest.

In 1504, Pope Julius II nominated Michelangelo Buonarroti as the artist in charge of painting the Sistine Chapel. Michelangelo's idea was to make, quoting Gianluigi Colalucci, "not simply a decoration of surfaces. On the contrary, by using painted architectural elements, Michelangelo wanted to include frescoes in Sistine chapel's architecture in order to modify without violating the chapel itself."[5] Indeed, three walls and the vault have painted architectural elements that frame biblical stories while the wall containing the *Last Judgement* opens itself outwards, having the sky as background. Despite

Michelangelo, *The Last Judgement*, Rome 1536-41.

the magnificence achieved by this work, the Church considered Michelangelo's frescoes, notably the *Last Judgement*, controversial and ambiguous.[6]

Debate during the Council of Trent (1545-63) focused on the subversive nature of Michelangelo's representation of the Church, not as the mediating element for deciding the destiny of those sent to Heaven or Hell. This non-canonical choice, although completely revolutionary, was his biggest shame before a Church ravaged by the rise of Protestantism.[7]

The *Last Judgement* painted by Giotto in the Scrovegni Chapel in Padua represents, by contrast, an example of what was considered the canonical way of representing this biblical story.

The painting, in fact, can be read on three different levels. The bottom contains, on the right, the Church and, on the left, Hell. At the middle level there is Christ with all the Apostles and on the top level Paradise, represented by Angels and Saints. The narration is hierarchical. The Church functions as the mediator, marking a clear distinction between those destined for Paradise and those destined for Hell.

While in Giotto's painting each element of the narration carries out a precise function, Michelangelo's *Last Judgment* expresses a completely different condition. By replacing the role of the Church as the mediator

of Christ on Earth with Christ Himself, Michelangelo wrapped the entire narration into an unstable and dynamic vortex where Just and Sinners, Saints and Demons are altogether.[8] There are no roles, no fixed functions and no hierarchy if not the one created by the new mediator, Christ, who is the pivot around which the vortex of bodies narrates the scene. Christ is the only one that plays an active role in the fresco.

In the rhizome with Parkour

Ultimately, if the *Last Judgement* in the Sistine Chapel represents the condition that emerges when a mediator is replaced with a new one, the discipline of Parkour explains the same sense of denial and replacement of mediator, this time in an architectural framework.

A training discipline that encourages unconventional methods of movement and travel within architectural space,[9] Parkour was invented by David Belle in 1988. In an interview on the occasion of the 2006 OSRAM Parkour World Meeting in Berlin, Belle explained the origin of this discipline. Inspired by his father, who was a high official in the French military fire service, Belle had been developing this practice since the age of seven by transforming military obstacle training into freestyle, holistic training. "We see the walls and passages that tell us: you should go like this or that. But we say: no, we can go like this just as well."[10]

Practitioners of Parkour thus become, with regard to walls, pipes, passages and, more generally, architecture function-shifters.[11] By doing so, they avoid any mediator, becoming the mediator themselves.

The way in which a building is used is always perceived of as a hierarchical set of relationships (the "instructions for use" explained in the prologue) that are sequentially called into question. For instance, to access their flats users must first open a main door. Then, they have to use stairs or lifts, establishing a second relationship. Finally, by opening the door of their flat, they arrive at home. In all these passages, main doors, stairs, lifts, etc. are all pieces of a sequence that produces a loop made by "axes of significance".[12] This loop reduces the user to a passive role. Without any stairs, the flat would be unreachable.

Practitioners of Parkour, in this regard, as function-shifters, deny these mediators by using pipes as lifts or balconies as stairs. They are inside a rhizome where there are no sequences of hierarchical passages and no pre-fixed routes. They decide from time to time how to arrive at their flats, following a more playful route.

Consequently, a building[13] becomes a rhizomatous map akin to the theories posed by Deleuze and Guattari. Balconies, pipes, overhangs, balustrades are points on this map "[that is] is reversible, [and] susceptible of constant transformation...".[14] The practitioner of Parkour continuously connects with these points. The connections in this view are not hierarchical but mutual. Like a

Giotto, ***The Last Judgement*,** **Padua 1306 ca.**

wasp and an orchid, a pipe temporary de-territorialises itself, becoming a lift. That is, the pipe changes its function for practitioners of Parkour, allowing them to go upwards. Practitioners, by doing so, re-territorialise the pipe. They re-establish its form, by lifting up towards their flat. By establishing this relationship, both the pipe-as-lift and practitioners of Parkour remain detachable and heterogeneous elements. The former, after having become a lift, keeps transporting its liquids, as well as the latter, after having used the pipe-as-lift, establishes a new relationship with some other element of the building.

Ultimately, from these analyses it appears that the real kernel of protest is not simply the one of denying mediation but rather how the latter is replaced. Protest suggests an inversion of roles, from a passive to an active one. While architectural space, through mediation, reduces users to a passive role, Christ actively plays in the painting as much as practitioners of Parkour do with buildings. That is, architecture can learn from protest to invert the relationship between building users and architectural space. This inversion of roles is at the heart of the following project, involving, on one hand, a concept of adaptive architecture and a transformative and resilient use of architectural space. On the other hand, the project suggests a liberation from traditional constraints to a new form of collaboration among figures who are involved in design processes - designers, users, institutional bodies, etc.

Project for an Urban Backdoor

The following project is a theoretical reflection, which through adaptive architecture and the use of a kinetic element, explores the inversion of roles in the relationship between building users and architectural spaces.

The Parioli[15] municipality issued a request for ideas for redeveloping an area between a train station, which links the north side of Rome with the north side of the Lazio region, and an ancient water source, probably attributable to Gian Lorenzo Bernini.

The theme, on which designers were invited to reflect, was the one of the urban door. This subject was mainly due to two different issues: a functional aspect of the train station and a cultural one of the source as historical trace, a memory of the place. It is exactly this binary condition that has stimulated our speculation on the proposed project as an urban backdoor.

On a global scale, the project proposes the creation of a green urban area between the source and the train station, in which the original condition of the source, as it was during the 17th and 18th centuries,[16] is recreated. The second part of the project is the replacement of the old train station with a new building which faces a second, new, mixed-use building. They are two signals, which enclose a void, a fringe where the urban backdoor takes place. This space in between is not only a

square, nor just a link between the two buildings but an infrastructure capable of providing an adaptive space for social interaction.

The urban backdoor

The pre-existent binary condition of the project site was inspirational for designing the urban backdoor. The site, indeed, oscillates between a cultural instance and a functional one. Rather than finding a compromise solution, a merging of opposites or a paradox, we opted for both poles.[17] We developed an algorithm that transforms the space in between the two buildings into something reactive.[18] The void becomes the backdoor, the infra-

structure capable of adapting itself to the different needs of the daily users.

The square is transformed into a four-piece kinetic[19] element which lifts up or down, accommodating the binary instance of being functional for train station users and, at the same time, a collective event generator. The kinetic mechanism is inserted into the pillars, which are inspired by the ones used in the Sendai Mediatheque[20] by Toyo Ito. The pillar is no longer just a static structural element that supports the beams, rather it becomes a clockwork within a dynamic system.

During the peak hours of operation when the passenger flow is high, a two-piece portion of the square (the functional instance) lifts up. One of the two pieces becomes a covered and welcoming space for train station users who arrive and depart daily while the other piece becomes a panoramic terrace, reachable from the cafeteria at the top level of the train station.

At off-peak hours of low passenger flow, the previous portion drops down to the ground to become a public square while the other two-piece portion (the cultural instance) lifts up. One piece becomes a space for collective aggregation while the other is an urban garden, accessible from the top level of the mixed-use building.

Movable glass panels, intended as multi-functional partitions, can be used as informative or art exhibition panels, as walls for stands in a local market, for video or movie projections and so on.[21] The aim is to realize a space that is neither open nor closed, neither inside nor outside, neither public nor private, but rather an adaptive space that embeds all these aspects.

(Un)Conclusion

A significant aspect of the project invites reflection on mediation in architecture, in which an architecture considers users in a different fashion and allows them to act as mediators themselves.

This new user's role suggests a dematerialisation of architecture, towards a more involved and interactive relationship with the collective: a dematerialisation which does not refer to physical architectural tectonic qualities, but rather to what characterises them and what is granted architectural functions and consequently typologies.[22]

In The Urban Backdoor, the possibility of transforming that space, of shaping it according to both the new users' role and needs, results in an adaptive type of architecture that avoids any functionalism. In this regard, the project articulates itself through an architectural space that does not impose its instructions for use to users. That is, through the use of a kinetic element, the resulting space is transformed into both a reactive and adaptive one. It is a kind of space that interacts with the collective and where the relationship between the latter and former is mutual rather than hierarchical.

TOP
Axonometric view of the project site

2,3,4,5
Perspective view of the new train station with the two-piece square lifted up

Finally, adaptive spaces can effectively turn users from passive actors to ones with active roles in architectural spaces. In such a scenario, two important changes must evolve to realize such adaptive architecture. First, a different way of managing architectural spaces is required with institutional and private bodies that should directly call into question the collective while setting daily or weekly programmes of events. The second aspect directly calls into question the role of architects and, more generally, practitioners. Adaptive architecture indeed suggests a devolution, from an architect who organises and instructs spaces to one who sets adaptive spaces that are transformable through the active intervention of the users.

These two aspects invite practitioners and involved bodies to explore a kind of architecture which, according to David Chipperfield, is composed of elements that do not stand as "individual spectacles but [they are] the manifestations of collective values, and the settings for daily life."[23]

ENDNOTES

1 Serres, M. 1982

2 Marc Augé, *Non-Places*, Second English language edition. ed.(London ; New York: Verso, 2008).

3 See also: Manuel DeLanda, "Beyond the Problematic of Legitimacy: Military Influences on Civilian Society," *boundary 2* 32:1 (Duke University Press, 2005).

4 In the book the Parasite, Michel Serres argues about the condition of space we can find in an airport. He says that "it is a space in the centre-milieu. It is deparasited and clean by obstacles so that it can be obeyed".

5 All the information related to the Sistine Chapel's frescoes are due to an interview that the authors personally had with Dr. Gianluigi Colalucci. He was leading the team that made the last restoration of Michelangelo's frescoes betwwen 1980 and 1989 and the last restoration of Giotto's frescoes in the Scrovegni Chapel. See also: F. Mancinelli, G. Colalucci, and N. Gabrielli, *Last Judgement*(Giunti, 1994). And Benjamin Blech and Roy Doliner, *The Sistine Secrets : Michelangelo's Forbidden Messages in the Heart of the Vatican / Benjamin Blech & Roy Doliner*(New York : HarperOne, c2008. 1st ed., 2008).

6 During the Council of Trento (1545-1563), the Church decided that the naked bodies in Michelangelo's frescoes, especially in the *Last Judgement* had to be covered up. In effect, many Saints were in ambiguous positions e.g. the head of S. Biagio standing behind S. Catherine naked was completely replaced while her body was totally covered up.

7 In effect, the way Michelangelo painted the *Last Judgement* describes a Protestant belief rather than a Catholic one.

8 Saints and condemned people are all together waiting to know their destiny. E.g. see how Martyrs are prostrated in front of Christ showing the signs of their martyrdom.

9 Defining Parkour properly is a hard task. Even David Belle and other formers of this discipline have never given a full definition of it. To have further information I would invite readers to see: http://parkourgenerations.com/article/parkour-history

10 David Belle interviewed in occasion of the 2006 OSRAM Parkour World Meeting in Berlin. Full interview is available at http://www.youtube.com/watch?v=YYwQLvIkQ88

11 See as a visual example French movies like *District 13* (where David Belle is one of the main character) or *Yamakasi* (the original group of nine practitioners of Parkour created by David Belle)

12 Gilles Deleuze and Félix Guattari, *A Thousand Plateaus : Capitalism and Schizophrenia / Gilles Deleuze, Félix Guattari*; Translation and Foreword by Brian Massumi(London : Athlone Press, 1988).

13 Parkour is practiced within any type of architectural space. The use of the word building here, although reductive for the practice of Parkour itself, is meant to give an address to the reasoning.

14 Ibid

15 Parioli is a neighbourhood located north side of Rome.

16 There are several Roman authors that describe the natural environment surrounding the water source. See for example: A. Nibby, *Analisi Storico-Topografico-Antiquaria Della Carta De'dintorni Di Roma*(Roma: Tipografia delle Belle Arti, 1837).

17 This is a legacy of Poststructuralism. See for example: Ferdinand de Saussure et al., *Course in General Linguistics*(New York: Columbia University Press, 2011). And Gary P. Radford and Marie L. Radford, "Structuralism, Post-Structuralism, and the Library : De Saussure and Foucault (English)," *Journal of documentation* 61, no. 1 (2005).

18 The algorithm was developed by using Grasshopper, a parametric plug-in for the 3d modeling software Rhinoceros. To have an overview see: http://www.grasshopper3d.com/

19 In this research field see for example the project for the Digital Water Pavilion for the 2008 Expo in Saragoza designed by Carlo Ratti Associati. (www.carloratti.com)

20 The Sendai Mediatheque was designed by Toyo Ito in Sendai, Japan. The citation of this building is due to the fact that it represents one of the first multimedia buildings. Pillars in the mediatheque are thought to be multimedia and connective elements rather than just pillars. See for example: http://www.archdaily.com/118627/ad-classics-sendai-mediatheque-toyo-ito/

21 Our proposal involved that collective was allowed to book spaces on the Urban Backdoor through the internet. In this way people could have decided on their own what kind of activity to do. This is akin to what theorized in Deleuze and Guattari, *A Thousand Plateaus : Capitalism and Schizophrenia / Gilles Deleuze, Félix Guattari*; Translation and Foreword by Brian Massumi. Notably the sentence: The ideal for a book would be to lay everything out on a plane of exteriority of this kind, on a single page, the same sheet: lived events, historical determinations, concepts, individuals, groups, social formations.

22 In this respect, the dematerialization is achieved by using an algorithm. From the *Oxford English Dictionary*, the term algorithm means to instruct a set of rules in order to provide a problem-solving solution for a system. That is to say, thanks to an a priori instruction for use, the project denies traditional architectural mediation and mediators' instructions for use

23 David Chipperfield in his opening speech from the last Venice Biennale 2013. Full speech is available at: http://www.labiennale.org/en/architecture/news/29-08b.html

CORAL TYPOLOGY

THE ARCHITECTURE OF TRANSFORMATION

by RICHARD GOODWIN

The idea of Modernism is over // past // pastiche
The idea of Post Modernism is over // rated // pastiche
Nature as a concept is Modernist
The idea of nature is over // rated // rotated

Architecture is landscape, which has a past
The idea of architecture is over // rated // rotated
War is Post Modernism
The idea of war is urbanism

Urbanism is Architecture // rotated
Modernism made good bones
The ocean is all history unrecorded // rotated
Architecture is the calcification of consciousness
Architecture is coral // rotated

Coral is a landscape // rotated
Coral is the new typology of urbanism
Urbanism is a coral reef // rotated

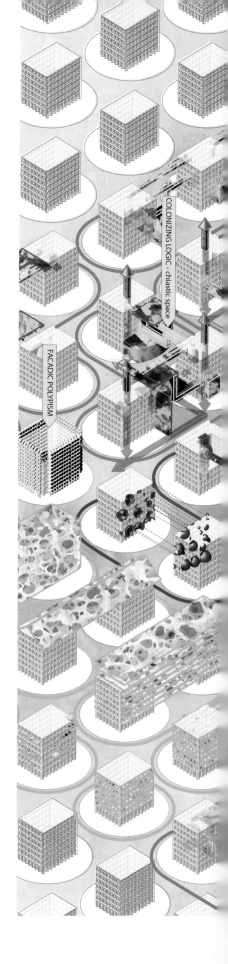

PARASITISM - tree inclusion

TECHNOLOGICAL POROSITY - water

ANAL ANGINE MECHANISM - core to skin

KINETIC ARCHITECTURE - skirt bifurcating

INTERSTITIAL INVASIONS - building weed

TECHTONIC BREEDING - fixed crane to structure

POROUS STRUCTURE - layered envelope

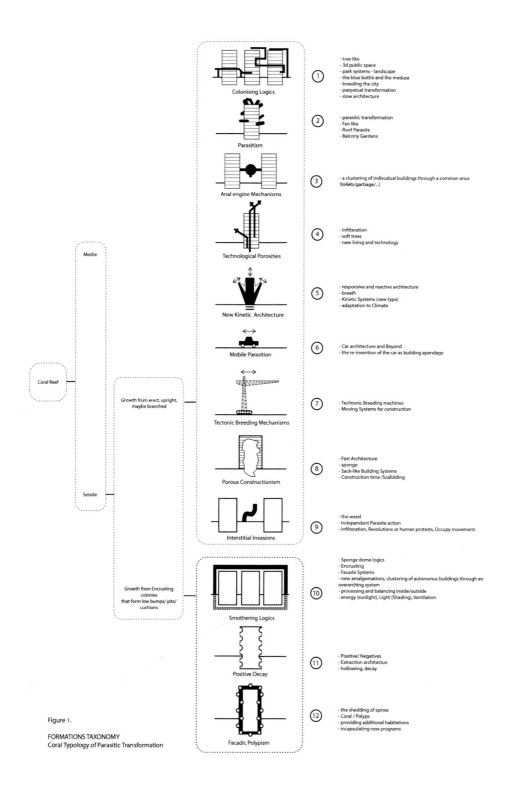

	Colonising Logics	① - tree like - 3d public space - park systems - landscape - the blue bottle and the medusa - breeding the city - perpetual transformation - slow architecture
	Parasitism	② - parasitic transformation - Fan like - Roof Parasite - Balcony Gardens
	Anal engine Mechanisms	③ - a clustering of indivudual buildings through a common anus (toilets/garbage/...)
	Technological Porosities	④ - Infilteration - soft trees - new living and technology
	New Kinetic Architecture	⑤ - responsive and reactive architecture - breath - Kinetic Systems (new type) - adaptation to Climate
	Mobile Parasition	⑥ - Car architecture and Beyond - the re-invention of the car as building apendage
	Tectonic Breeding Mechanisms	⑦ - Techtonic Breeding machines - Moving Systems for construction
	Porous Constructionism	⑧ - Fast Architecture - sponge - Sack-like Building Systems - Construction time /Scafolding
	Interstitial Invasions	⑨ - the weed - Independent Parasite action - Infilteration, Revolutions or human protests, Occupy movement.
	Smothering Logics	⑩ - Sponge dome logics - Encrusting - Facade Systems - new amalgomations, clustering of autonomus buildings through an overarching system - processing and balancing inside/outside - energy (sunlight), Light (Shading), Ventilation
	Positive Decay	⑪ - Positive/ Negatives - Extraction architectue - hollowing, decay
	Facadic Polypism	⑫ - the shedding of spines - Coral / Polyps - providing additional habitations - incapsulating new programs

Figure 1.

FORMATIONS TAXONOMY
Coral Typology of Parasitic Transformation

Introduction

Coral reefs form the edge condition of certain continents, exhibiting exquisite fragility and complexity of life. They are a metaphor for the complex equation of transformation within all natural systems. This article posits that coral typologies can provide a set of imaginative resources, metaphors and experiments for grasping and reimagining the changing nature of cities in the 21st Century. Fundamental to this argument is the belief that a system of complex and continuing transformation of existing structure (buildings), within cities, is more desirable than seeking the cleared site or the modernist "tabula rasa". Urban development is perpetually in a state of becoming, forming the architecture of accumulation within the age of contingency, despite Modernism's attempts to create permanent order. Hence it follows that the city is like a coral reef and as such needs re-classification that has an equal complexity to that of our complex environment with all its current dilemmas. Coral Typology is as much an experiment as it is a true typological study of the architecture of transformation. In particular, this vision of the city, and classification of its ongoing transformation, concentrates on building additions and subtractions to existing structure, which prejudice the idea of retaining building envelopes and using their "bones" as building blocks for the next solution to social, spatial and urban planning needs. This idea draws from six years of research conducted in Sydney, Beijing and Shanghai. It is put forward not only as a possible new architectural typology for city buildings to guide the future, but also as a methodology of design and urban planning which is fundamentally about transformation as the best sustainable design practice.

Fundamental to the following text is a belief in the need to redefine the nexus that continues between architecture and art. Coupled with this condition is a belief in the gravitational forces between Modernism and what some might call the age of contingency.

I define architecture as part of the fine art spectrum as opposed to the pedagogical Bauhaus notion of architecture being the mother of the arts. Modernism allowed a disjunction to occur between so called fine art and architecture, which we are still in the process of redressing.

Why? Because the full spectrum of art practice gives architects all the tools they need for change. Historically they include: Appropriation, Metaphysics, Surrealism, Chance, Poetry, Performance, Futurism, Cubism, Expressionism, Conceptual Art, Minimalism and so on. Func-

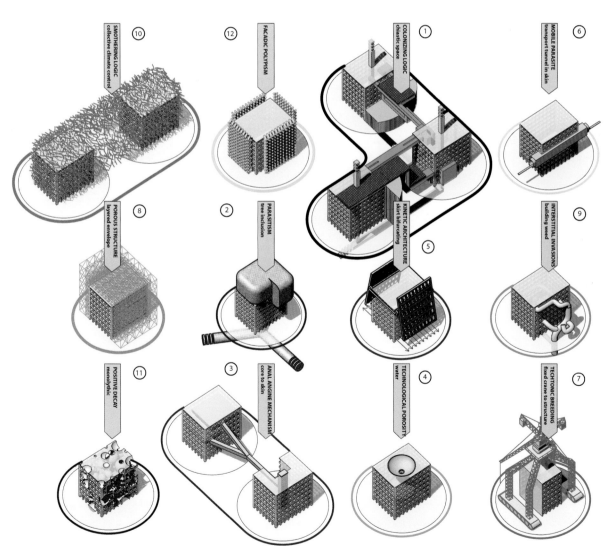

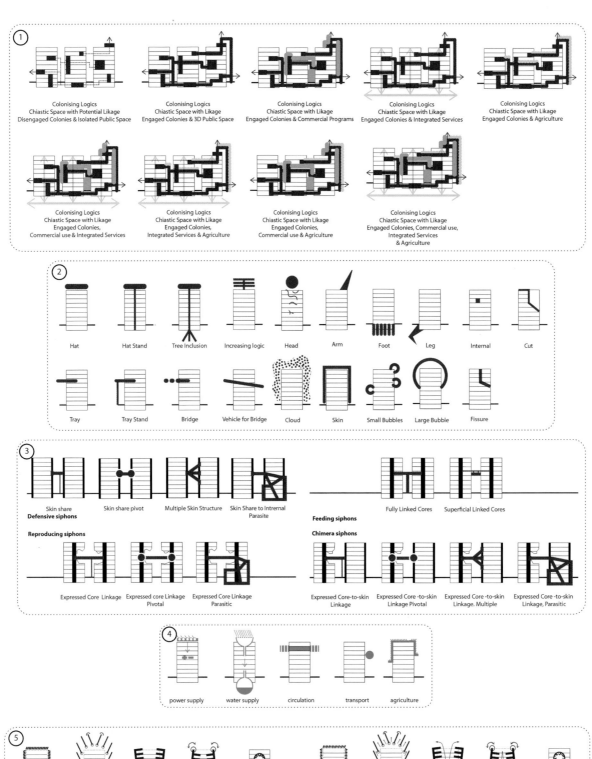

1

Colonising Logics
Chiastic Space with Potential Likage
Disengaged Colonies & Isolated Public Space

Colonising Logics
Chiastic Space with Likage
Engaged Colonies & 3D Public Space

Colonising Logics
Chiastic Space with Likage
Engaged Colonies & Commercial Programs

Colonising Logics
Chiastic Space with Likage
Engaged Colonies & Integrated Services

Colonising Logics
Chiastic Space with Likage
Engaged Colonies & Agriculture

Colonising Logics
Chiastic Space with Likage
Engaged Colonies,
Commercial use & Integrated Services

Colonising Logics
Chiastic Space with Likage
Engaged Colonies,
Integrated Services & Agriculture

Colonising Logics
Chiastic Space with Likage
Engaged Colonies
Commercial use & Agriculture

Colonising Logics
Chiastic Space with Likage
Engaged Colonies, Commercial use,
Integrated Services
& Agriculture

2

| Hat | Hat Stand | Tree Inclusion | Increasing logic | Head | Arm | Foot | Leg | Internal | Cut |

| Tray | Tray Stand | Bridge | Vehicle for Bridge | Cloud | Skin | Small Bubbles | Large Bubble | Fissure |

3

Skin share Skin share pivot Multiple Skin Structure Skin Share to Intrrenal Parasite

Defensive siphons

Fully Linked Cores Superficial Linked Cores

Feeding siphons

Reproducing siphons

Chimera siphons

Expressed Core Linkage Expressed core Linkage Pivotal Expressed Core Linkage Parasitic

Expressed Core-to-skin Linkage Expressed Core -to-skin Linkage Pivotal Expressed Core -to-skin Linkage. Multiple Expressed Core -to-skin Linkage, Parasitic

4

power supply water supply circulation transport agriculture

5

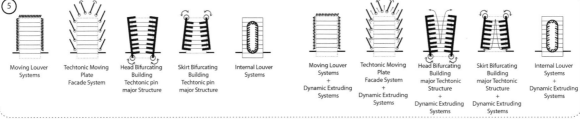

Moving Louver Systems Techtonic Moving Plate Facade System Head Bifurcating Building Techtonic pin major Structure Skirt Bifurcating Building Techtonic pin major Structure Internal Louver Systems Moving Louver Systems + Dynamic Extruding Systems Techtonic Moving Plate Facade System + Dynamic Extruding Systems Head Bifurcating Building major Techtonic Structure + Dynamic Extruding Systems Skirt Bifurcating Building major Techtonic Structure + Dynamic Extruding Systems Internal Louver Systems + Dynamic Extruding Systems

Coral Typology Of Parasitism: Expansion Of Taxonomy

tion and program do not free architecture from poetry. When they do, we end up where we are. We need to call on the past and future to save the present.

Despite the leadership of the Russian modernist movement and the work of artists from Malevic to Duchamp, architecture defied its conceptual roots. At the birth of Modernism we find the text of Adolf Loos "Crime and Ornament", a call to arms for those believing that through architecture, which does away with decoration, lies a path to civilization, while through art one becomes mired in anal eroticism, to use Freud's terminology.

To quote Hal Foster:
""Ornament and Crime" was published in the same year as "Character and Anal Eroticism", where Freud first writes of the Anal character... In a sense, Freud states directly what Loos implies indirectly: on the one hand, that art involves a sublimation of sexual energy, implicitly of anal eroticism....; and on the other, that civilization is founded in a renunciation of this sexuality supported by a reaction against anal eroticism"

This predicament and separation, dictated in some ways by Modernism, led to the structures of functionalism, which despite the advent of Post Modernism and Deconstruction still drives city architecture today. It can be argued that Minimalism finally put a stop to neo-classicism's indulgences in the past. However the purity of Minimalism rendered it a powerful "full stop". Ironically it is now reborn endlessly as a decorative surface or series of applied systems, as a result of this power. When art and architecture form one spectrum of a divergent art practice, as they did for the Russian Constructivists, then it is my argument that we will move forward. It is not a coincidence that this typology is written by a practicing artist/architect.

Within the legacy of the Situationists, and their beloved architect Constant in particular, we find a thread, born of Dada, which leads to a prejudicing of the social construction of cities over the rational matrix of modernism. It is art's particular ability, as illustrated by the Situationists, to critique the city and treat it conceptually as a plastic materia, that has led to an understanding of the city as an organism. From Dada to the Situationists, to Archigram, to Gordon Matta-Clarke, to Lebbeus Woods, Chris Burden and Vito Acconci, hybrid art/architecture practice has dealt with the deficiencies of modernist architectural practice.

This thread also informs my practice. Through Constant and his "Unitary Urbanism" concept, we see the grid of modernism change theoretically into the "Dynamic Labyrinth" of fluid and changing architectural program via an eternal "derive".

It can now be argued that the Situationist's dream of Unitary Urbanism and the vision of a future swapping work for play became manifest as the internet rather than built space. This remains a cause and effect provocation to physical architecture on which this study builds.

The Coral Typology attempts to breathe life back into the old socialist lungs of the Situationists.

To quote Constant:
"This entirely new situation (New Babylon) incites us to a new interpretation of construction that goes in an opposite direction to the way that once led to functionalism. The ideology of constructivism – parallel to that of socialism – is no longer bound to the idealization of labour, but on the contrary will lead to the liberation of the former labourer from the need of production, the liberation of the laboring masses whose creative forces until our time have been wasted in activities that were simply necessary to keep mankind alive."

I don't believe that we will finally get to play on mass within a new Babylon, however we are already seeing the phenomena of movements such as "Occupy", the Arab Spring uprisings and art actions titled "Social Sculpture" emerging. More than ever before the movement towards "multi-disciplined professional teams" designing our cities and our interest in the social construction of cultures and multi-cultures is leading us towards an understanding of cities which embraces the DNA and urgency of slums – seeking solutions in their terms rather than via static modernism.

This typology calls for social porosity in the face of post 911 paranoia and closure of buildings to the public space edge. Porosity has proven that types of public space exist within private space (Chiastic Space), which needs to be accessible within cities, for healthy social construction to exist. In the current move from Modernism to the socially objective "Age of Contingency", this closure is the enemy of public space and transformative "building to building" connections, which this Typology aspires to. This movement away from Modernism occurs today within the current trend of politics beyond ideology. We live in the age of post- political "bio-politics" to quote Slavoj Zizek.

"Post-political is a politics which claims to leave behind old ideological structures and, instead, focus on expert management and administration, while "bio-politics" designates the regulation of the security and welfare of human lives as its primary goal. ...That is to say, with the depoliticized, socially objective, expert administration and coordination of interests as the zero level of politics, the only way to introduce passion into this field, to actively mobilise people is through fear, a basic constituent of today's subjectivity."

I consider that this tendency towards post political urban planning, which sees only closure and surveillance as an answer to security, is an enemy of the typology I am proposing. It desires closure not "Porosity" and connection, which could feed culture and social cohesion.

To date security tools and systems, which render architecture impervious and beyond connection, have not predicted terrorist events but have merely setup mechanisms for successful forensic analysis after the attack. These systems also maintain the status quo and consolidate a view of Architecture as a literal bastion of Capitalism or ownership. To succeed in the prevention of this closure, the "Occupy Movement" needs to be nomadic, like a Situationist army, and politics should return to a system for developing ideologies. The city can be an engine for this via its places of debate – public space.

Fundamentally Coral Typology seeks to balance the equation between public and private space. In promoting this equilibrium our cities will develop multiple ground planes and an interconnectedness, which becomes the architecture of invagination. Existing cities, now encrusted with the high-rise structures of the 20th Century, may be like sunken ships awaiting coral reef transformation in their next lives. Fundamental to this argument is the belief that the system of transformation of existing structure (buildings) is the way forward for a large percentage of architecture in the urban context.

The complexity of the classification of life forms within coral reefs has been and is an immense ongoing enterprise by scientists. This study has chosen to use the key reef protagonists within its chosen groups and types. The analogy or metaphor of coral, for types of parasitic transformations of existing architecture, was sought as a tool or "way in" to the problem of classifying new building types and extensions within our city organisms. The conceit of this study is to assume that within the universe complexity mimics complexity as seen in "Chaos Theory". All natural systems eventually converge – all therefore hold the key to transformation. The revolution or "rotation" is located in the idea that all potential sites of building form and transformation are necessarily three-dimensional. Boundaries and public space must be rotated and three dimensionalised in order to understand the future of density. Urban planning has been dictated to by 2D's maps floor space ratios and plot ratios for too long. Each site is an envelope bounded by six two dimensional sides making a three dimensional volume.

Possible connections to adjacent buildings and to the ground or field outside of the site will affect all six sides. This revolution in urban planning, via porous boundary envelopes above and below ground, offers rewards for such connections. If licensed connections are made using new urban planning instruments, and if they serve the purpose of the city in making three-dimensional existing public space, then the city's blood and oxygen supply is enhanced.

Hence the need for a predictive typology of building, which encourages a revolution in urban planning by radically transforming existing structure.

The typology is broken into twelve formations within the Coral Reef. The classification of these formations is drawn from a wide range of generally accepted scientific information. It is not specifically referenced as the types have been collated and re-formed into convenient and generalized descriptions. This re-ordering is a reaction to the scientific system, convenient to my intuition and imagination, but defying quotation in the academic sense.

The Coral Reef exists in two major forms – Motile or disconnected and Sessile or connected. This study is formed through the Sessile System.

1. Colonising Logics (Polyp Colonies)

Each individual polyp (the molecule of this typology) is morphologically and functionally specialized and lives as an individual. It lacks an exoskeleton (human analogy).

Despite this apparent autonomy, the individual polyps are strongly integrated with each other, to the degree that the colony attains the character of one large organism.

There are three different colonial structures for these life forms:

1. Stolonal colony: a root-like extension of the body structure.
2. Unright colony: upright and irregularly branched structure.
3. Siphonophore colony: a floating colony structure composed of polyps and medusas (the reproductive form).

This category is pivotal to the overall typology as it forms the base organizational structure of a Coral Reef.

Colonizing Logics, as a principle, sets out to extend and make the city more complex through the idea of three-dimensional public space and its effect on the programs and densities of building groups.

2. Parasitism (Plumate Zooids)

The reef colony is composed of individual polyps housed in separate tubular or box like shells and shell systems such as "moss-lace" (gridded networks of shell forms) which form a host body.

Parasitism understands the logic of the city as a series of possibilities for adapting the host body of buildings. The parasite acts like an individual, which takes advantage of the three dimensional grid and its units, to occupy and to transform. It is possible for the parasite to be symbiotic as opposed to destructively and selfishly parasitic.

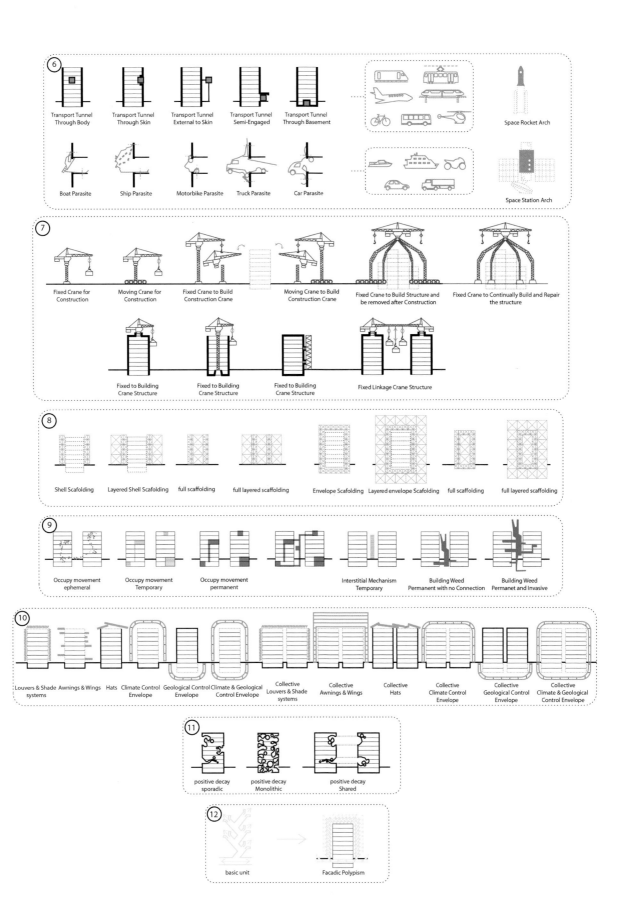

6

Transport Tunnel Through Body

Transport Tunnel Through Skin

Transport Tunnel External to Skin

Transport Tunnel Semi-Engaged

Transport Tunnel Through Basement

Space Rocket Arch

Boat Parasite

Ship Parasite

Motorbike Parasite

Truck Parasite

Car Parasite

Space Station Arch

7

Fixed Crane for Construction

Moving Crane for Construction

Fixed Crane to Build Construction Crane

Moving Crane to Build Construction Crane

Fixed Crane to Build Structure and be removed after Construction

Fixed Crane to Continually Build and Repair the structure

Fixed to Building Crane Structure

Fixed to Building Crane Structure

Fixed to Building Crane Structure

Fixed Linkage Crane Structure

8

Shell Scafolding

Layered Shell Scafolding

full scaffolding

full layered scaffolding

Envelope Scafolding

Layered envelope Scafolding

full scaffolding

full layered scaffolding

9

Occupy movement ephemeral

Occupy movement Temporary

Occupy movement permanent

Interstitial Mechanism Temporary

Building Weed Permanent with no Connection

Building Weed Permanent and Invasive

10

Louvers & Shade systems

Awnings & Wings

Hats

Climate Control Envelope

Geological Control Envelope

Climate & Geological Control Envelope

Collective Louvers & Shade systems

Collective Awnings & Wings

Collective Hats

Collective Climate Control Envelope

Collective Geological Control Envelope

Collective Climate & Geological Control Envelope

11

positive decay sporadic

positive decay Monolithic

positive decay Shared

12

basic unit

Facadic Polypism

Coral Typology of Parasitism: Expansion of Taxonomy

4. Technological Porosities (Gorgorian Colonies)

Gorgorians are composed of individual polyps. Like a tree, Gorgorians are structured through an internal central skeleton and have branches. The branching system has several structures being dichotomous, lateral, pinnate and interconnected. As opposed to trees, these colonies do not attach themselves to a hard substrate and instead anchor themselves in mud or sand. Gorgorians are filter feeders.

The supple tree-like forms of the Gorgonian Polyps function as the ideal diagrams for infiltration. Translated from the coral reef to the city, these Gorgonian Colonies form new technological conduits for the city. Whereas the logic of Porosity is to find complex three-dimensional pathways for public space, these Technological Porosities enable old structures to be literally re-wired and/or re-filtered.

5. New Kinetic Architecture (Barnacle Buildings)

Barnacles are composed of small plates enclosing a soft body. Inside the shell, the barnacle consists primarily of long segmented legs, intestines and stomach. The body of the Barnacle possesses a kind of cement, which creates an extremely adhesive substance that sticks the barnacle onto the rock. Adult barnacles are protected by four, six or eight calcareous plates, which form a volcano like cover.

The Barnacle has been chosen within this typology as the model for all new independent or stand alone architectural entities. As a model for new building, the Barnacle provides us with the ability not only to self sustain but also to introduce dynamic kinetic responses to site and atmosphere, which enhance their ability to do so. The ability for the tech-tonic plates of buildings to respond to all conditions adds a new meaning to adaptive and sustainable design.

6. Mobile Parasition (Mussel Byssus)

Mussels anchor themselves to hard surfaces though thread-like elastic substances called "byssus". They are bilaterally symmetrical and laterally compressed. They are filter feeders and feed on planktons and other microscopic sea creatures.

Cars, trucks and trains are mobile parasites within the city. To imbue them with architectural systems and programs is to take the next step in the transformation of the city. The Mussell encourages further thinking in relation to a kinetic architecture, which has its own systems for energy and waste management. The umbilical connection of the mussel to the coral reef system in the form of the Byssus is yet to be thought in relation to the car and its building host. The Byssus could also be the freeway and road systems now divorced from building program and design.

3. Anal Engine Mechanisms (Siphon systems)

Siphons prefer artificial structures such as wharfs, pilings and boat hulls as an environment.

The colonial structure of siphon systems is either social or compact.

In the former the siphons have a solitary form but are interconnected through a basal stolon. In compound colonies each member has its own brachial siphon but shares a common arterial siphon with several other siphons arranged in a ring.

Within the coral reef, these clusters of individual organisms can share an anus in specific groupings. In relation to the typology this idea lends itself to the development of independent waste and energy systems within groupings of buildings. Whether generating their own waste systems or creating completely independent waste systems, the sharing of power and waste between buildings is an engine for change, which defies barriers.

**Governor Phillip Tower Sydney with Parasite attachments
designed as a response to the research 2005**

7. Tech-tonic Breeding Mechanisms (Pedal Disk Anemones)

A sea anemone is a single large polyp. Anemones have no structural skeleton. Instead they have a hydrostatic skeleton: they stand upright through the balance of their contractile cells pulling against their central gastro-vascular cavity. Anemones hold themselves through their muscular pedal disc on which they can move.

The sea anemone is both a giant polyp and an independently moving machine. Its hunting and building action makes it strong. Moving around the reef it regulates the movement and attraction of living organisms. Its application within the typology embraces the military and policing systems of the city.

8. Porous Constructionism (Branching Construction Sponge)

Sponges are the most primitive animals within the reef, as they lack proper organs and have no definitive shape. The main opening of a sponge is used as an exit to expel waste.

Sponges are composed of 3 types of cells. The outer cells are flatter and epidermal, the inner cells move constantly and produce water currents that flow though the pores into its central cavity and out through the upper opening of the body.

Like the sponge, construction scaffolding, used in the process of building, has no definitive shape. This aid to construction, providing access, forms nests around the activity of construction. This ephemeral and "fast architecture" is very porous and useful also for social cohesion in relatively short periods of time.

9. Interstitial Invasions (Crown of Thorns Starfish)

This particular reef animal is a large multiple-armed starfish that usually preys upon hard corals. The starfish preys on coral by digesting the surface of living tissue from the coral skeletons. These skeletons persist, together with the mass of coralline algae that is essential for reef integrity.

The Crown of Thorns Starfish is a destructive parasite on the coral reef if conditions allow it to proliferate. In such conditions it becomes a "weed". Within this typology there is a need to define actions that are inherently destructive. Whether they are describing wars, revolutions or "Occupy Movements". These interstitial infiltrations create new architectural possibilities via destruction of existing systems and occupancy. Fundamentally this type is assigned to the mechanisms of war.

10. Smothering Logics (Encrusting Sponges)

The structure of Encrusting Sponges is highly complex. Encrusting Sponges have no central core, and instead their cavity is highly branched and is divided into clusters of small round or oval chambers. The overall form of the sponge is indefinite due to its maze of water channels. Different chambers within the sponge operate in parallel rather than in series leaving no food in the filtered water.

The Encrusting Sponge provides a compelling metaphor for the continual re-appraisal and re-design of the façade systems of high-rise buildings in the city. This is fundamental to any notion of transformation, which improves both the energy equation and sustainability of the architecture. Over time all city towers will be subject to changes in their façade systems, which in turn are responsible for the filtration of their environments.

11. Positive Decay (Moss-Lace Systems)

The moss-lace system is a colony of animals within the coral reef system. The colony is diverse and complex in structure and is composed of individual modules or zooids, and each zooid is effectively a complete animal. Nevertheless, the zooids remain interconnected and may exchange nutrients and other substances through interconnecting cables of minute pores in their body walls. The colonies usually form sheets covering rocky bottom (algae).

Decay in architecture needs to be read as a positive system. The extraction of parts of buildings is as transformative as the addition of parasites. Extraction within the geology of architecture is in fact the building of new forms.

12. Facadic Polypism (Branching Encrusting Systems (Hard Branching Systems))

A hard coral is a colony of genetically identical polyps. Hard corals might be perforate or imperforate in structure. Perforate structures have a porous skeleton, which allows for polyps to connect with each other through the skeleton. Imperforate corals have a hard solid skeleton. The polyps are extremely interconnected by a complex and well-developed system of gastro-vascular canals, allowing significant sharing of nutrients and symbioses.

Hard corals are the major reef architects. Polyps, the living portion of corals, extract calcium from seawater and combine it with carbon dioxide to construct the elaborate limestone skeletons that form the reefs backbone.

Facades with new program form another type of smothering logic. Whether it is through urban agriculture, additional balconies or new shade making devices, Facadic Polypism turns façade systems into independent architecture—"Thick Skins".

Conclusion

The diagram to the left depicts parts of the Sydney CBD growing new parasitic forms of public space connections based on ten years of research. This "Porosity" research is outlined in my book *Porosity: The Architecture of Invagination*. The images form the conclusion—an image of what the typology might mean.

JAPAN'S ARCHITECTURAL GENOME

DESTRUCTION AS A CHANCE FOR RENEWAL

by IRIS MACH

Throughout the centuries, Japan has encountered many crises of both manmade and natural origin – be it economic and cultural, foreign invasions, wartime destruction or recurring hazards like earthquakes, typhoons and tsunamis. Due to this history, Japan has developed a building culture that embraces, rather than shuns, decay and destruction as an integral part of its system.

This approach is rooted in both Buddhist and Shinto religions, which regard destruction and renewal as basic principles of life. A well-known example of this concept is the Shinto Ise shrine, which is ritually dismantled and re-erected every twenty years. In this way, the process of natural decay is anticipated and preemptively counteracted. Likewise, many residential and commercial buildings in Japan are conceived for a lifespan of just a few decades.

The Japanese Metabolist movement of the 1950s-70s similarly addressed the issue of decay in the field of architecture. However, rather than completely demolishing and rebuilding a structure in one go, it regarded a building, as well as the city as a whole, as a living organism that should be designed to be replaceable cell by cell in a constant, ongoing process.

Furthermore, Japan has always striven to assimilate foreign expertise into its culture. This approach has supported the continuous renewal of traditional concepts and brought Japan to the cutting edge of building technology also in the field of disaster mitigation.

Based on these principles – preemptive, sustainable demolition as a means of preservation and slow, constant regeneration and transformation – Japan may serve as an example of how to anticipate, counteract and recover from various crises, while recognizing their potential for renewal.

Aerial view of the two adjacent building sites,
the Naikù shrine the Shinto Ise shrine compound in Mie

Japan's passage through collapse and extinction

In 1968, the Japanese architect Arata Isozaki, then in his late thirties, was invited to contribute to the Milan Triennale. Although a member of the international board, his presentation centered largely on Japan in the wake of Hiroshima's devastating destruction. His intention was to display the collapse and (re-)construction of Japanese architecture and urban space in analogy to the human life cycle:

> Though the architect and urbanist are dedicated to progress, it is nonetheless impossible to escape altogether a recurring premonition of total collapse. The basis of architecture is construction, and urban space is understood as its extension. But over against such ideas as had long persisted in Western thought, I intended to pose the example of Japan's passage through collapse and extinction[1].

One of his main exhibits within the multimedia installation *Electric Labyrinth* was a mural entitled *Hiroshima Ruined Again in the Future* depicting the devastated city landscape after the atomic bomb, including some likewise destroyed future building structures. This tragic image of total annihilation was to him the symbolic starting point for the dramatic transformations and the complete regeneration of postwar Japan in social, economic, cultural and architectural terms, which had since taken place – destruction, to him, was the origin of renewal.

The case of Ise Jingu

At the time of the exhibition only about 20 years after the end of the war, however, Hiroshima as well as the almost equally destroyed Tokyo had already recovered and turned into modern, flourishing cities.

What is the key to this resilience and rapid regeneration regarding both man-made and natural catastrophes? Perhaps surprisingly, one clue can be found in the case of the well-known Shinto Ise Jingu shrine compound, located in the Mie prefecture in southwest Japan and dedicated to the sun-goddess Amaterasu. It is considered one of the holiest sites of Shinto religion and is closely linked to the Japanese imperial family. The whole sanctuary consists of more than 120 shrines in the city of Ise and the surrounding area, out of which the two main buildings – Naikù (Inner Shrine) and Gekù (Outer Shrine) - have been ritually dismantled and rebuilt identically in new materials alternating on two adjacent sites in a cycle of twenty years since 690 AD. The old materials are recycled and donated to other shrines, thereby closing the circle of sustainable reuse.

On the one hand, this ceremony enacts a symbolic sequence of death and rebirth in religious terms – on the other hand, it anticipates the natural process of decay of the wooden structure and thus ensures the permanent newness and seeming eternity of the building. This practice has made Ise Jingu an icon of Japanese architecture, epitomizing its appreciation

"Tokyo Bay Project" by Kenzo Tange, 1960, unrealized.

of ephemerality and de-/reconstruction as a cyclically recurring progression.

The Metabolists
In contrast to stone or brick cultures, Japan as a wood-building culture has to deal with the significant impermanence of its traditional construction material. Interestingly, however, the same strategy was also transferred to contemporary buildings made out of much less ephemeral substances, such as steel or concrete.

The Japanese Metabolist movement, officially founded in 1960 on the occasion of the World Design Conference (WoDeCo) held in Tokyo, consciously referred to Ise Jingu as the "archetype of Japanese architecture"[2] and an inspiration for its futuristic concepts of "living/biodynamic" architecture in terms of constant alterability and impermanence[3].

Looking for solutions to the urban crises caused by Japan's explosive economic growth and its unstable and scarce land, the group looks to historical Japanese precedents - the cyclical rebuilding of Ise Shrine and the modular growth of Katsura Detached Palace - as inspirations for a new type of changeable architecture.[4]

The Metabolists claimed that architecture should be as adaptable as a living organism, in order to be able to react to the constant, even disastrous, changes in its surroundings – whether technical, economic or natural:

Buildings and cities must be able to adapt, grow, elevate, even float, if they are to survive the dual pressures of rapid modernization and inevitable natural change (usually calamitous).[5]

In contrast to Ise Shrine, however, the buildings should not be completely dismantled and rebuilt in anticipation of damage or decay, but be replaced bit by bit in a slow but constant process, according to necessity. The most iconic tangible project, among many unrealized futuristic visions, was Kisho Kurokawa's "Nagakin Capsule Tower" for residential and office use, completed in 1972 in Tokyo – an "aggregation of [144] individual unit spaces", mounted onto two cores. Each of the capsules was a self-contained and easily detachable entity, prefabricated by a company for shipping containers. As such, the building represented an accumulation of loosely connected cells, which could be exchanged one by one in case of requirement.

The same approach was to be applied to the city as a whole, substituting the buildings at regular intervals, while retaining the basic organizational structure. This idea was promoted on the basis of futuristic city concepts like the "Tokyo Bay Project" by Kenzo Tange and later Kisho Kurokawa, which proposed a grid-like floating superstructure spanning the whole bay of Tokyo. Yet, its origins were grounded in the custom of

constructing rather short-lived/temporary houses due to the experience of recurring catastrophes:

many Japanese buildings have been destroyed by fires, earthquakes and war. They have been repeatedly replaced by extremely short-lived buildings. For example, in the Edo period (1603-1868), most ordinary townspeople lived in rental housing. The risk of disaster was so high that landlords only built small, flimsy houses whose cost could be recouped in five to six years. This is related to Metabolism. The metabolic cycle – that is, the lifespan – of houses was extremely short by European standards. According to a government report in the [19]'90s, the average lifespan of a Japanese house is only 26 years[6].

Also in this case, it was the prospect of disaster that gave rise to radical renewal.

Learning from pagodas
Ise Jingu was not the only historic role model for contemporary Japanese architecture – the field of constructive disaster mitigation was equally influenced by traditional building techniques.

When Tokyo lost about 140,000 inhabitants and about 50% of its buildings in the blaze following the great Kantō earthquake in 1923, it became clear that the then prevailing wood constructions were ill-suited to such a dense agglomeration. In search of new

Photo, Pagoda of the Horyù-ji Temple compound in Nara

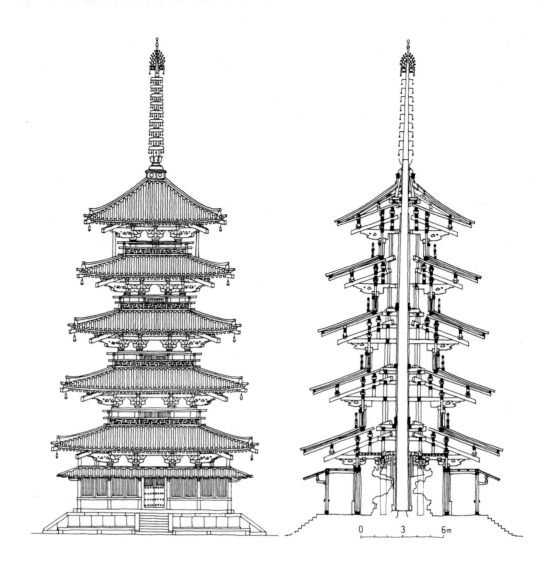

0   3   6m

building materials steel became an option; it was more durable than wood and noncombustible, but still allowed the continuation of the building tradition of skeleton structures.

Fathoming the possibilities of new construction techniques, stimulations were taken from established historic buildings. The new building type of the skyscraper had for example been inspired by historic pagodas, which had proven especially resilient to earthquakes[7]. One of them is the famous Horyùji pagoda in Nara (32,5m), which dates back to 594 AD, making it one of the oldest existing wooden buildings in the world.

The key to this durability lies mainly in the central pillar (shin-bashira), which acts as a damper to the oscillations of the loosely piled stories devoid of any rigid connection. In case of the high-rise building, this concept has been translated into a central core, connected to the surrounding floor slabs by means of oil dampers. Recent examples of this structural solution can be found e.g. in the "Mode Gakuen Cocoon Tower" in Tokyo[8] , the "Mode Gakuen Spiral Towers" in Nagoya[9] and the "Tokyo Sky Tree"[10].

This concept of combining traditional Japanese know-how with modern Western technology has significantly contributed to renewing the Japanese building culture and became known under the term "wakon-yôsai" ("Japanese spirit – Western technology").

The architectural genome

As described, Japanese cities have experienced many significant alterations born out of crises, but one source is often overlooked - the influence of foreign cultures that started with the opening of Japan in 1868 after more than 200 years of self-imposed isolation (Sakoku). Tokyo in particular seems to have changed completely in the past 90 years after the disastrous Kantò earthquake in 1923, the severe destruction during WWII and the subsequent rebuilding under Western influence.

When the architectural historian Hidenobu Jinnai set out to explore Tokyo in the late 1980s, he was intrigued by the extent the city had actually been altered during the past centuries. Comparing the current metropolis to historic maps, he was surprised to realize that the change was in fact mainly superficial. Although there was hardly any building dating back more than 100 years, the underlying structures of high and low cities, transportation routes, merchant's quarters and more had mostly been retained[11]. His discovery that Tokyo's organization had been typologically preserved confirmed an earlier Metabolist remark:

> *In the same way as life, as organic beings composed of changeable elements, as the cell, continually renewing its metabolism and still retaining as a whole stable form - thus we consider our cities. [Kenzo Tange][12].*

In comparison, Ise Jingu appears rather hieratical in its stolid replication of identical form. However, on closer inspection the differences are diminished: research has shown that even the seemingly transfixed formal codes of the shrine have been subject to minor alterations throughout the centuries. Proportions of building parts have been transformed, metal fixtures added or omitted and even the layout of the buildings on site has been changed throughout the centuries according to the prevailing taste. In this light, the ritual "rebirth" of the building appears as an organic process:

> *More than anything else, Ise may recall the mechanism by which life forms sustain their identities: selection from a pool of genes in response to certain external conditions[13].*

This may be the clue to the resilience and adaptability of Japanese architecture: the materiality and form of buildings as well as cities is rather incidental – instead, it is the "architectural genome", the underlying structural information, which is preserved and interpreted afresh with every rebuilding.

Thus, destruction is much more than merely an ending: it is also part of a cycle, giving way to a novel beginning and a chance for renewal.

ENDNOTES:

1 Isozaki, Arata, and David B.Stewart. 2006. *Japan-ness in architecture*. Cambridge, Mass: MIT Press, 84.

2 Koolhaas, Rem, Hans-Ulrich Obrist, Kayoko Ota, and James Westcott. 2011. *Project Japan: metabolism talks*. Koln: TASCHEN GmbH, 19/227.

3 Ibid,175.

4 Ibid, 185.

5 Ibid, 175.

6 Ibid, 227.

7 cf. Fujita, Hanazato and Sakamoto, "Earthquake response monitoring and seismic performance of five-storied timber pagoda".

8 Mode Gakuen Cocoon Tower: 204m, 2008, owner: Mode Gakuen, design: Tange Associates/Paul Noritaka Tange, structural design: Arup, contractor: Shimizu Corporation; cf. Minami, "Mode Gakuen Cocoon Tower – An Iconic High-rise Campus in a Dense City".

9 Mode Gakuen Spiral Towers: 170m, 2008, owner: Mode Gakuen,

architectural and structural design: Nikken Sekkei, contractor: Obayashi Corporation, cf. Yamawaki and Kobori, "Mode Gakuen Spiral Towers – An Approach to Structural Design for Realizing Advanced Structural Configurations in Earthquake-prone Countries".

10 Sky Tree: 634m, 2012, developer: Tobu Railway, architectural and structural design: Nikken Sekkei, , contractor: Obayashi Corporation, cf. Nikken Sekkei, "Structural Technology".

11 Jinnai, Hidenobu.1994. *Tokyo: a spatial anthropology*. Berkeley: University of California Press, 8.

12 Koolhaas, Rem, Hans-Ulrich Obrist, Kayoko Ota, and James Westcott. 2011. *Project Japan: metabolism talks*. Koln: TASCHEN GmbH, 197.

13 Isozaki, Arata, and David B. Stewart. 2006. *Japan-ness in architecture*. Cambridge, Mass: MIT Press 138.

Tokyo Sky Tree completed in 2012, 634m

2400 block of Jefferson Street Philadelphia, PA, 1928.

IN BETWEEN

PLACES OF RESILIENCE IN THE POSTINDUSTRIAL CITY

by SALLY HARRISON

Philadelphia: Workshop of the World

In a span of less than fifty years Philadelphia's industrial economy built neighborhoods and sites of production that earned the city its renown as the Workshop of the World. Singular in purpose, efficient in design and fuelled by immigration, the neighborhoods of central North Philadelphia built in the second half of the 19th century were part of a machine for working.[1] The spaces of everyday life were subsumed in a vast, densely occupied grid, interrupted only by ribbons of manufacturing and rail lines. North Philadelphia in 1900 bore little resemblance to Penn's vision of "greene countrie towne" with its humanizing pattern of public squares; for more than a half century it was a massive profit center, but in C.S. Hollings terms, "an accident waiting to happen".[2]

The rapid build-up of these workers' neighborhoods was mirrored by their spectacular collapse a century later, transforming what had been "ghettos of opportunity" for immigrant populations into "ghettos of last resort" for the African American migrants from the rural South.[3] Until the 1950's central North Philadelphia maintained its population with its built fabric intact, but its period of seeming stasis was followed by a cycle of disinvestment, depopulation and physical decay. Exogenous forces and internal rigidities that had been gathering since the 1920s - suburbanization,

rising social inequity, the growth of the highway system and changes in manufacturing processes and in patterns of consumption - were poised to take a mighty toll on both the industrial economy and the urban environment that was built expressly for its operation. Between 1951 and 2000 North Philadelphia neighborhoods were utterly transformed.

The district's decline can be understood as the outcome of a poorly elaborated urban ecosystem, over-specified in its origins and function, and ill-equipped to adapt quickly to critical change. Space for the "living systems"– the more fluid social, cultural or natural accretions- had been underrepresented or suppressed in the roll-out of the rigid, disciplined gridiron of neighborhoods; absent was the spatial complexity supporting overlapping smaller patterns of human use[4] that are the natural engines for regeneration.

Yet even as blight has eroded large districts in the postindustrial city, the spatial fragmentation has opened up opportunity for resilience, for change and innovation at smaller scales; places of beauty, humanity and utility have gradually grown into the un-built spaces. These tactical and locally driven adaptations have begun to accumulate and trickle up to form new urban typologies. One can make an analogy between Holling's understanding of ecological resilience and the

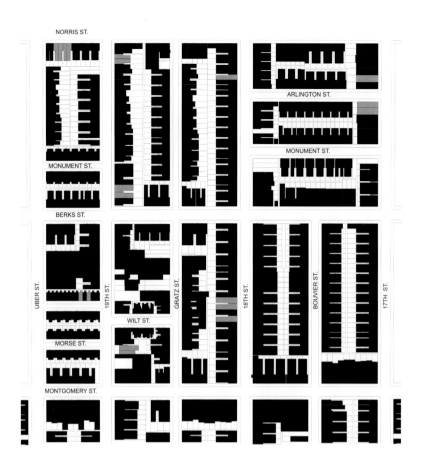

1951
The Urban Workshop
@ Temple University

VACANT PROPERTY
OCCUPIED PROPERTY
UNBUILT

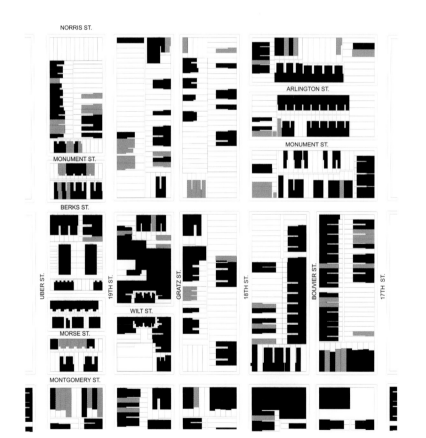

2000
The Urban Workshop
@ Temple University

VACANT PROPERTY
OCCUPIED PROPERTY
UNBUILT

TOP
1951 Occupancy / Vacancy map, showing a cluster of residential blocks; the fabric intact. The Urban Workshop.
BELOW
2000 Occupancy / Vacancy map, showing a cluster of residential blocks; the fabric deeply eroded. The Urban Workshop

qualities needed for social resilience in remaking the urban context. He uses the term "panarchy" to describe the condition of a complex and healthy system where there is a continuous multi-scalar interaction between rapid innovation and slow moving conservation.

The panarchy summarizes succinctly the heart of what we define as sustainability. The fast cycles invent, experiment and test; the slower ones stabilize and conserve accumulated memory of past successful, surviving experiments. In a healthy system, each level is allowed to operate at its own pace, protected from above by slower, larger levels, but invigorated from below by faster, smaller cycles of innovation. The whole panarchy is therefore both creative and conserving. The interactions between cycles in a panarchy combine learning with continuity.[5] Adaptations of existing row housing to current living patterns, urban farming collectives like the Glenwood Greenacres Gardens and public art initiatives like the Village of Arts and Humanities have worked imaginatively with residual, in-between conditions to address social, economic, cultural and health needs of the neighborhood residents. These represent the "back loop" of Holling's adaptive cycle where "the previously accumulated mutations, inventions, external invaders, and capital can become re-assorted into novel combinations, some of which nucleate new opportunity."[6] This is a dynamic balance that may model for North Philadelphia a strategy for second growth.

Dwelling form: Adaption versus Erase and Replace
The North Philadelphia neighborhoods have been the preoccupation of urban policy since the mid-twentieth century when Urban Renewal schemes sought to eradicate and remake the fabric, long neglected and increasingly inhabited by the poor. Slum Clearance programs followed by the construction of high density towers sought to "solve" the problem only to become, famously, failed concentrations of poverty and attendant social ills. Only a few decades later this misguided pseudo-Modernist idea was replaced with yet another top-down policy. Towers were taken down. This was attended by carnival crowds at the spectacular demolitions. Now the issue of depopulation compounded the problems of uninhabitable public housing projects and a new program of "engineered resilience"[7] was conceived by the city of Philadelphia to respond to lowered density. In heavily eroded row house neighborhoods families were relocated (again) and vast tracts of land cleared for development that would be implemented by private developers who required economies of scale to profit. As if to remediate poverty by changing the dwelling image, new suburban-style homes sprouted with low density, car-centric site plans. Convenient as means of disposing the surfeit of excess land, the homes sit on huge un-useable back yards. An "as-if" feeling

pervades these spaces; they bear little resemblance to Philadelphia and carry with them none of the pre-existing culture embedded in place. Even now planners have begun to doubt the value of this inner-city sprawl, as it undermines public infrastructure of transit, commerce and other institutions.

Yet a closer investigation of small-scale interventions in the eroding context provides clues as to how a more socially and ecologically resilient system can emerge. In Dalabor Vesly's words: "It is possible to start with a given reality of any existing city and to discover, in most of them a residuum of tradition sufficient to support a consistent, imaginative, and sometimes even radical reinterpretation of the status quo.[8] All over North Philadelphia imaginative residents and small community-based developers have engaged the "given reality" of the fabric, finding a "residuum of tradition" in which to reweave the fractured residential landscape rather than replacing it whole cloth--adapting the row house, appropriating the residual open space and reinterpreting the block typology to respond to contemporary needs for spacious homes, places to play and relax and park the car, and building sites for neighborly affiliation.

Habitat for Humanity has been building a community one block at a time over three decades; its work is "inefficient by design". Respectful of the human context, it draws into its process those who have lived in the neighborhood, the patterns of daily use, and the existing built fabric. An old multi-bay garage housing its workshop and offices forms a visible presence of on-going productive activity, its projects gradually circling out from that center, holding the re-emerging neighborhood

Proposal for the Village Campus. The Urban Workshop, lead designers 2012. Clockwise from top left: the Village Workshop and Craft Courtyard; the Design Arts and Exhibit Building expanding the Germantown Avenue storefront; Performing Arts Building opening onto Ile lfe Park; the Sound Studio and Arts Business Incubator; Dwellings and Artist Residences; The Herb Garden and Environmental Learning Center.

together. With hands-on participation of home-owners, volunteers and professional staff, the organization renovates houses large and small, joins tiny homes together, and in-fills vacant lots with new construction.

Their largest project to date combines these strategies to reweave and reinterpret the existing structure of a deteriorated block. The" given reality" consisted of three and two story homes, some occupied, some vacant interspersed with large patches of open space. Adapted to contemporary dwelling patterns, new row homes – wider, shallower, more open to the social and natural environment than the old - fill in theses spaces. But, unlike their pseudo-suburban counterparts, these projects do not undermine Philadelphia's essential identity. They maintain the materiality, rhythm and continuity of the street.[9] The narrow mid-block alley found in the traditional row house block, having lost its value, has been adapted as well, expanded to create a new spatial typol-

ogy. Now it forms an inner courtyard connecting house backs and their private yards. Parking requirements are met, but the space functions on a social level. A new kind of contained porosity emerges in the neighborhood fabric, a safe place for children to play casually observed, and a site for informal neighboring. This appears to be a robust contribution to the neighborhood structure. In Franks and Stevens terms a "loose space", it slips between private and semi-public domains adding a new layer to the dwelling experience, increasing the depth of neighborhood affiliations.[10] As one resident put it, "I have my street neighbors and then I have my backyard neighbors. We know each other in different ways."[11]

Glenwood Green Acres Garden
Sitting on his front porch Tom Williams surveys the lush Glenwood Green Acres, a four acre allotment garden that stretches along the deep Amtrak rail siding across

Glenwood Green Acres Gardens, Philadelphia

from his home. It has flourished at the center of North Philadelphia for thirty years.

> I am too old to be out there now but we had a time of it getting (the garden) started. There used to be a big whiskey factory right there that employed a lot of people around here, but they closed down and the building just stood there for years falling apart. Kids would go and play inside but it was dangerous. We kept asking the city to tear it down, and they ignored us till a body was discovered; the next day they were out with bulldozers... Next, people come at night and dump all sorts of trash and debris, and we were fed up. Two other fellas and I thought we'd start a garden – not just a backyard garden, but like a city farm. We'd grown up in the South, so we knew what we were doing. We could give our kids something of our experience.[12]

Within three years the entire site was appropriated with ninety plots that, with support from the Pennsylvania Horticultural Society, yielded vegetables, fruit and flowers, and over the years neighbors built garden sheds and a pavilion and planted an orchard along the rail tracks. The garden, like a swarm, operates simultaneously on the individual and the collective scales, with a modest set of rules for participation, and a rotating steward.[13] Though chiefly a productive landscape for individual gardeners, it has evolved locally as an intensely used social space for barbecues and informal gatherings, and as a hybrid institution offering horticultural workshops and intergenerational projects on the heritage of southern agriculture. Far from the single-purpose, hierarchical model of industrial development that originally formed the site, this enterprise emerged from the bottom-up, a creative response to a complex overlapping set of needs: to remediate large scale blight, to reconnect with cultural heritage, to support household economy, to improve nutrition, to engage natural systems, to work socially. The site which, in the industrial period, had been a model of what Henri Lefebvre calls "exchange value" has been transformed as a place of "use value"[14] that comprises the "features of oeuvre, of appropriation". It is both shared and productive.

Glenwood Green Acres' innovative adaptation of the derelict urban land has trickled-up to engage, inform and reinvigorate the urban structure. It has attracted gardeners not only from nearby residential blocks but also those from neighborhoods outside North Philadelphia, who might not have had reason to venture into this community. Together they contribute a percentage of each lot's yield to non-profits dedicated to hunger relief, helping further to nest the garden within the larger social networks of the city. And to defend the garden from the encroachment of developers, the Pennsylvania Horticultural Society has formed a land trust for its long-term preservation for community gardening. The

diverse scales of interest that engage Glenwood Green Acres form a healthy system like Holling's panarchy in which "each level is allowed to operate at its own pace, protected from above by slower, larger levels, but invigorated from below by faster, smaller cycles of innovation."

As Philadelphia continues to struggle with its surfeit of vacant land, and as the "locavore" and healthy foods movements have taken hold, the city considers agriculture as an important use inside its borders. Glenwood Green Acres is a model of resilience. The continuous, disused, formerly industrial rail sidings offer a broad ribbon of open space that can accommodate a new urban typology at both the neighborhood and city scale. This suggests the potential for significant intervention, aggregating locally operated farms, markets and greenhouses along the path that has blighted and fragmented the city for decades.

The Village of Arts and Humanities
> As necessary as science, but not sufficient, art brings to the realization of urban society its long meditation on life as drama and pleasure. In addition and especially, art restitutes the meaning of the oeuvre giving it multiple facets of appropriated time and space...

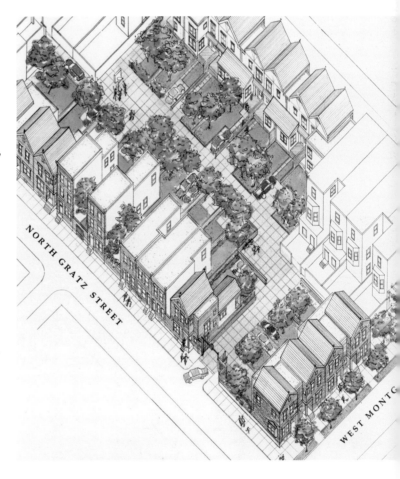

Habitat housing, Philadelphia, Axonometric showing the weave of old and new

Ten blocks east one finds another place of resilience; here space vacated in the postindustrial period has been in various ways appropriated for art. The site is a study in continuous adaptations to changing physical, economic and cultural circumstance through which a hybrid institution has emerged.

In 1969 Arthur Hall the director of the Afro-American Dance Ensemble found space for his organization on a vacated 19th century storefront on Germantown Avenue, a bustling neighborhood shopping corridor, intact but beginning to experience the effects of disinvestment and decay. While in Philadelphia, Hall taught West African dance and culture to thousands of children and adults, and toured nationally and internationally. When funding from federal and local government programs precipitously declined in the 1980's, Hall left Philadelphia –but not before engaging a young artist Lily Yeh to create a park on several recently opened lots next to the storefront studio. Yeh worked with local residents to build the Ile Ife Park on appropriated land, and over three summers it was completed. When Hall's studio closed, he left her the storefront building to carry on a community-based practice, and the Village of Arts and Humanities was founded.

Yeh gathered around her neighbors of all ages and began the work of land transformation. In its first decade, the Village evolved incrementally in counterpoint to the eroding residential context, weaving into a three block area adjacent to Germantown Avenue, a breathtaking network of mosaic–filled parks, passages and gardens. A holist sense of place was embedded here, integrating social and spatial change and creating the oeuvre that Lefebvre speaks of. Teaching and learning were contingent to the park building practice, and various programs of Africanist dance and drumming carried Hall's legacy forward, often filling the newly created interstitial spaces with sound and energy.

The Village received international and national recognition and foundation grants flowed in. The organization dramatically expanded its scope and ambitions in the next decade, undertaking new art parks and more complex land development projects. But these were scattered about the community, disassociated from place of origin, and the Village struggled with its organizational capacity. Indeed, as praxis yielded to production, a kind of internal rigidity, inherent in project generation, set in. In its expansion the Village was quietly becoming a victim of its own success, and the unexpected shock of the economic downturn that began after 9/11 and worsened throughout the decade, left the organization bereft of resources from the larger systems that had nurtured it. Even its charismatic founder left.

Most of the outlying projects foundered, though the artwork still stands as if inviting future imaginaries. But even in the well-integrated core area the network of muralled parks and gardens became underused as the housing fabric that held them together underwent a second accelerated collapse, losing a third ofits residences by 2010. Intimate parks that had been nested among rows of homes, now stood out in the open, still beautiful, but untethered from context, transforming the Village from a place where the "in-between" was energized by daily life to ghost-like vestige.

As new land transformation initiatives came to a halt, and the Village's original residential context eroded, it seemed to have lost its unique integration of art and life. Despite this, the Village was able to rebound – slowly – in evidence of the filtering and conserving process of the adaptive cycle. As Holling says, "The fundamental paradox is that change is essential, and yet stability is necessary." Art education programs begun in the period of Arthur Hall now began to flourish taking on a life of their own, fulfilling an exceptional need to provide at-risk teenagers a place to experiment

LEFT
Village of Arts and Humanities, Philadelphia. Angel Alley. Lily Teh, lead artist. 1994.
RIGHT
North Philadelphia row housing, railroad tracks and industry cheek by jowl, Philadelphia, PA

with creative processes. No longer attached to a park-building program, new forms of expression and creativity – videography, graphic and fashion design, hip hop, creative writing, art entrepreneurship and environmental education– have begun being taught to an ever-increasing number of young people, as schools no longer can provide this type of education.

Seeking to build up the spatial capacity for emerging year round programs, a new initiative has been undertaken. The loss of so many dwellings, a kind of creative destruction, has opened up large spaces in the Village core allowing new ideas to emerge. The three-block Village core is reconceived as a community institution, a campus for diverse modalities of creative education. No longer a project of filling the voids, the Village seeks to create a new context built on the fragments of the old. A vision plan draws together and reinvents the threads of the past adapting the residual pattern of residential fabric, developing Arthur Hall's community-centered art education programs, and building upon the extraordinary infrastructure of art space laid down by Yeh and her cadre.

In the plan, new and renovated program spaces are distributed strategically throughout the site creating an inter-connected campus layered with diverse, overlapping subsets of activities. The existing parks and gardens, their murals, sculptures and low defining walls, are reenergized with adjacent purposeful activity. Existing row buildings– some homes, some used by the Village- are supported, maintaining the scale of the original 19th century fabric and forming the internal spine. Porosity, color, tactility, nature- all these qualities of the original Village vision- inform the new interventions, ground the programs, and reconnect them to their context. The Village has gathered to it partnering organizations that will develop and occupy sites within the emerging campus, building a sustainable eco-system of diverse participants nested within a larger whole. In small tactical increments the work of the next generation has begun; it is tending toward Holling's "front loop" of the adaptability cycle, to stabilize, conserve and integrate.

Conclusion

It is a legacy of the industrial city that the in-between - the places of loss, vacancy and emptiness - are the very spaces where the human spirit can often flourish and act with purpose and imagination. The lived world proceeds at its own pace, creates its own narratives of place and is rich in content for change-making often invisible to the instruments for policy-making. The rush to remake places whole cloth, so satisfying from above, undermines the wealth and complexities that accumulate on the ground and seep into in the rifts and holes in the eroded context. Despite the losses endured in North Philadelphia's postindustrial decline it is indeed

fortunate to have retained enough of its fabric – both physical and social – to provide a framework for a resilient urban ecology that can incubate tactical creative responses to the city's changing aspect. Connecting these local Initiatives to the larger systems can both sustain the small scale innovations and energize the established slow-moving cycles of culture, economy and urban development. If given both time and an ethos of shared making, postindustrial city neighborhoods can evolve toward a more sustainable, beautiful and human paradigm.

ENDNOTES

1 Sam Bass Warner, *The Private City: Philadelphia in Three Periods of its Growth*, 2nd Edition, (Philadelphia: University of Pennsylvania Press, 1987), 52-53, 201-206

2 L. Gunderson, "Resilience and Adaptive Cycle," in *Panarchy : Understanding Transformations in Human and Natural Systems*, L. Gunderson and C. S. Holling (Washington, DC ,London: Island Press, 2002) 45.

3 Carolyn Adams, et al., *Philadelphia Neighborhoods, Division and Conflict in a Postindustrial City*, (Philadelphia: Temple University Press, 1991), 1.

4 Christopher Alexander, "Planning: A city is not a tree," in *Design* 206 (1966): 46

5 C. S. Holling, "Theories for Sustainable Futures," *Conservation Ecology* 4,no.2 (2000), http://www.consecol.org/vol4/iss2/art7/

6 C. S. Holling, "Understanding the Complexity of Economic, Ecological, and Social System," *Ecosystems* 4, no. 5 (2001), http://www.jstor.org/stable/3658800

7 Jianguo Wu. and Tong Wu," Ecological Resilience as a Foundation for Urban Design and Sustainability" in *Resilience in Ecology and Urban Design : Linking Theory and Practice for Sustainable Cities*, ed. Stewart T.A. Pickett, M.L. Cadenasso, and Brian Mc-Grath (New York: Springer, 2013), 211-230.

8 Dalibor Vesley, *Architecture and Continuity* (London: Architectural Association, 1982), 12.

9 David Hinson and Justin Miller, *Designed for Habitat*, (New York: Routledge, 2013), 118-131.

10 Karen A. Franck and Quentin Stevens, "Tying Down Loose Space, " in. *Loose Space: Possibility and Diversity in Urban Life*,ed. Karen A. Franck and Quentin Stevens (New York and London: Routledge, 2006). 1-34.

11 Sally Harrison, "Inefficient by Design: Habitat for Humanity In North Philadelphia," in *Proceedings of the 2010 I ARCC/EAAE International Conference on Architectural Research: The Place of Research / The Research of Place*, ed. Richard L. Hayes and Virginia Ebbert. (Washington: Architectural Research Centers Consortium, 2012), 451-460.

12 Tom Williams, interviewed by Sally Harrison, Philadelphia, PA, July 26, 2013

13 Patricia H. Hynes, *A Patch of Eden : America's Inner city Gardeners* (White River Junction, VT : Chelsea Green Publishers,1996)

14 Henri Lefebvre, "The Right to the City," in *Writings on cities / Henri Lefebvre*, ed. Eleonore Kofman and Elizabeth Lebas (Cambridge, Mass : Blackwell, 1996), 124. Op. Cit. 156-157

Unité d'Habitation, Firminy-Vert, A Close-up View from the Roof-terrace

FOSTERING RESILIENCE IN A VULNERABLE TERRAIN[1]

by PARI RIAHI, PHD

The deteriorating banlieues of Paris are violent and dysfunctional. Within these suburbs, les Cités HLM[2] shelter some of the most vulnerable citizens of the large metropolitan. Resisting change partly due to their fixed built conditions, these cités call for major repurposing. What possible transformations in long and short terms can build resilience in these volatile environments? The majority of the difficulties associated with the cités are in many outside the realm of the built environment. Yet, being preoccupied with the abrupt changes between the inside and outside, and the individual and collective in these large housing projects, this paper asks the question of what may be doable within the territory of the design disciplines to help improve these seemingly rigid structures and the vulnerability that lies underneath.

In our collective imagination, the underprivileged suburbs of Paris are often associated with bouts of violence, car burnings and drug trafficking. Beyond these widely mediatized images, it is hard to form a tangible image of les banlieues as living environments. The size, density, urban policies and governance of Paris intra murous and that of its larger surroundings, have historically contributed to staggering differences. In referring to some of these differences, Simon Ronai suggests that the case of Paris presents an "anomaly" as the city is both "geographically and symbolically" separated from its adjacent communities.[3] He claims that these differences are at the root of a domination and exploitation pattern imposed from the city onto its suburbs. The differences, which are exaggerated to the point of making the suburbs into walled-off, prison-like environments in the action movie *B13*,[4] are nonetheless real enough to create an invisible barrier between the two sides of the Boulevard périphérique.

To properly enter into the realm of the cités HLM, the paper gathers elements from four distinct sources to construct a body of evidence and form a hypothesis. First, a book by writer and sociologist Azouz Begag, who interviewed over a hundred adults previously residing in the suburbs, is looked at. Second, a memoir by Samira Bellil, a young woman who lived her life in a Parisian *banlieue*, is considered. Third, a movie by Abdellatif Kechiche that takes place in the Seine-Saint- Denis banlieue is examined. Ultimately, a particular HLM, the only one of Le Corbusier's Unités d' Habitation to have operated as such until 2003, is referred to. These seemingly diverse sources are brought together to form a body of evidence from different times and places. Focusing on one of the most symptomatic problems of the cités, that of isolation and separation, which exists at multiple scales and specifically on the lack of proper spaces of gathering, are the central themes of the present study.

THE PROMPT: FROM PHYSICAL SEPARATION TO ALTERNATIVE MODES OF INHABITATION

In *Les Derouilleurs*,[5] a book based on over a hundred interviews conducted in 2000 and 2001, Azouz Begag, tracks the path of previous inhabitants of difficult neighborhoods who left the suburbs behind. Begag argues for a necessary *déclic* (a prompt / a trigger), which enabled those inhabitants of the cités HLM to move away and take residence elsewhere. Qualifying the life in those environments as morose, he suggests that it was necessary for these people to leave the projects in order to get exposed to other forms of physical, social and cultural life.[6] Begag's argument is both fascinating and problematic from the point of view of the built environment. On the one hand, his thesis claims for a physical displacement and separation, allowing the individuals to become conscious of the limits of the environment they have lived in. On the other hand, a physical distanciation

is neither possible for all of the cités' inhabitants, nor would it be effective at such a massive scale.

Begag's hypothesis corresponds with the memoire of Samira Bellil, as she recounts her life in a *banlieue* of Paris.[7] Bellil's parents had immigrated to France from Algeria. Her early years were spent in Belgium in foster care, prior to returning to live with her family. She was subjected to gang rapes as a teenager and had to battle physical and psychological traumas for years until she came through with the help of a psychotherapist. She published her memoire in 2002, and became an advocate for her "sisters in distress".[8] Contemplating her life in Belgium, she describes it as "gentle and peaceful.... a healthy normal life, close to nature... ."[9] Reflecting on the possibility of remaining in Belgium, she states: "If I have stayed... I never would have become the Beurette of the banlieue; the little tramp who sunk herself in hassles and misfortune."[10] She then identifies her return to France as a pivotal moment, causing her an emotional and environmental shock: "I see myself crying, bawling even. I am in the hall of a sad gray building. There are broken mailboxes, strong odors of a musty basement, and lots of garbage."[11] She concludes that episode by indicating her parents' address as the ultimate indicator of the life that awaited her: "...they lived in a *banlieue*, The Parisian suburb of Saint Denis. A dreary apartment with dreary parents."[12] In these passages and throughout the book, it becomes clear that in Bellil's eye, the change of environment is tied very closely to her change of a life style.[13]

A counterpoint to Bellil's story is a movie entitled *L'Ésquive* by Abdellatif Kechiche, presenting a more nuanced image of the inhabitants of the cités. In *L'Ésquive*, a group of adolescents practice an episode of one of Marivaux's plays, entitled: *Le Jeux de l'Amour et du Hazard* (Games of Love and Chance) for their French literature class. The movie was filmed in 2002 in the cité des Franc-Moisins in Seine-Saint-Denis department. Krimo, a teenage boy of Maghrebi origin develops feelings for his classmate Lydia and conjures up a scheme to play the role of Arlequin opposite her, wishing to express himself through Marivaux's words. Kechiche weaves the narrative of the original play with the unraveling of Krimo and Lydia's feelings towards each other. The juxtaposition of these two sets of realities with the cités HLM as the backdrop creates an assemblage of spatial, linguistic and behavioral images that are unprecedented. While the story toggles back and forth between the enclosed interior spaces and the bleak setting of the projects in the outside shots, the weight of the cités is an ever-present force within the visual, audible and emotional core of the story. As the movie brings to life the inarticulate fragility of Krimo and the forceful energy of Lydia, we witness the manifestation of a different type of prompt. The play rehearsed times and again throughout the film, turns the open space at the foot

Unité d'Habitation, Firminy-Vert, View of the West Elevation Loggias

of the towers into a field within which emotions come to life. The seemingly ubiquitous public space, similar to the launching pad of Bellil's gang rape, pulsates with alternative possibilities. In addition to claiming a space, the play extends its territory to developing a complex linguistic fabric, in which the dualities of the 18th century French merge with the suburban slang, where poetries of different sorts are brought together into a tenuous, yet potent cohabitation.[14]

   In both of these narratives the dwelling units are meant for solitude and refuge, while the outside becomes the open field for interaction with others. The fragility occurs at the onset of these two worlds colliding into each other. It is the lack of multiple thresholds that turns this transition from the inside to the outside, and from the individual to the collective problematic. Returning to the possibility of introducing a *déclic*, I suggest expanding the notion of a prompt to the spatial realm. The idea of a flexible space, transformable into an alternative environment, in which more than one activity may take place, can offer a relief from the narrow scope of possibilities within the cités. I propose that physical distanciation and categorical separation can be replaced with building programmatic and spatial flexibility within the dwelling unit and on the terrain

that surrounds the projects might prove more effective. From the point of view of the built environment, the connection between the inside and outside seems to be the most critical and also potentially attainable area of focus. Spatial prompts may be physical artifacts placed within or added to an already existing place or can take the form of programmatic strategies, leading to alternative perceptions of a place or a momentary break from the environment that surrounds one in the cités. The question therefore becomes the following: How can these immediate spaces at the foot of the towers be turned into safer, less threatening environments? How can the public spaces that are supposed to connect and filter the many individuals living in these mid/ high rise towers turn into more amenable environments?

   These questions lead us to revisit Le Corbusier's Unité d'Habitation in Firminy. This particular Unité, which was built to be an HLM from the inception was never fully occupied and in the 1980s the northern portion of the building was closed down, relocating the inhabitants to the southern portions.[15] I visited the building frequently over the years of 1997-98 to document the life of its inhabitants.[16] In my view some of the elements in that project are reciprocal with the idea of spatial prompts, either as physical objects or as pro-

Unité d'Habitation, Firminy-Vert, View of the Playground from the Roof-terrace

grammatic devices creating in-between spaces, already realized and therefore tested to a certain degree. The eerie glazed wall dividing the building in half made the *rues intérieures* less convincing than originally intended, and the much-debated pilotis were never as populated or controversial due to the isolation of the tower on the hill. However three particular places/elements are potential contenders for spatial prompts: the loggias, the toit-terrasse and the école maternelle.

On the inside of the dwelling units, the space that offers room for detachment and individual expression is the space of the individual terraces, which opens on the *séjour* (living room). Demarcated by a small ledge, the loggia becomes an extension of the living area or acts as a terrace allowing for some separation. The double height window of each loggia frames both the living room and the master bedroom mezzanine and modulates light and view at once, expanding the overall perception of space within each unit. The articulation of the loggias on the exterior façades expresses slight variations of use, demarcating each unit while maintaining an overall identity of the whole. While balconies or terraces exist in many of the projects, they often turn into un-identifiable buffer zones with minimal potential for inhabitation. In Unité, the loggias become significant elements, in allowing one to identify with a larger outside entity, all the while bearing the possibility of using the space as an outdoor room, or the extension of the indoor one.

Destined for individual or collective use, the *toit-terrasse* serves as a viable option for either isolation from the others or togetherness at the scale of the building. This shared common ground links the individual to a larger community and environment, establishing a continuous visual connection and providing isolation at once from other buildings. Its paradoxical placement reverses the dynamic of the public spaces as one that is constantly in plain sight, and offers a sense of shelter and individuality at the scale of the building. The possibility of inhabiting the environment at a scale that allows for continuous visual connection with physical isolation makes it possible to identify one's living space with a larger sense of community. Here the sense of belonging that is made possible is not through the identification of a number, a postal box, or a door in a corridor, but by the ability to be part of a larger community, while still being confined to some measure of security. In comparison, the play area/ amphitheater-like space of the building is more amenable to small children and in full sight; the *toit-terrasse* offers a possibility for shielding one from other's eye, while being public space. As a counterpoint to the space of the pilotis, the roof offers views and an opening to the larger cityscapes that makes it an entirely different experience. In its half abandoned state, the roof of Firminy's unite still fostered possibilities of spending time, in solo or in small groups for its inhabitants.

L'école maternelle (the kindergarten) presents the possibility of allocating communal space, destined for a specific use and tied to domestic life within the projects. While Corbusier's original idea corresponded more with creating independence and autonomy that had to do

Unité d'Habitation, Firminy-Vert, Scenic View from the Roof-terrace

with self-sufficiency, the possibility of creating a series of non-contradictory functions that can co-exist with housing is one that is both relevant and possible.[17]
In creating a gradation from the private to public, the *maternelle* served as a destination for the families who lived in the building and created a unique itinerary, undertaken at fairly regular intervals that allowed for activities other than going home or getting out of the building. One can imagine that the inclusion of such programs can create networks within the cites that do not require building of extremely costly infrastructure or buildings, but have to do with the reconfiguration and allocation of small incisions of program within the projects to make for patterns of use and circulation in addition to the already existing buildings.

Conclusion

Bellil's narrative best captures the extreme extremities of highest introversion/ isolation and the uttermost extroversion. Her story identifies the solitude, the thrill and the fear that are associated with the projects at once. This polarity is also present in *L'ésquive*. We often find Krimo at home or out at the foot of the building, spending time with his friends. In Kechiche's movie, the house acts as a place of retirement, solitude and reflection, and the classroom, a space of exposure to forces and opinions, still presents a measure of positive environmental control. It is the space of the amphitheater that truly acts as the stage in which the range of the teenagers' spirits ebb and flow with some freedom. The main difference between Bellil's narrative and the spaces represented in the film lies in the existence of this liminal space, which offers a possibility to engage with others still at an intimate scale. Kechiche epitomizes the thin threshold between hope and fear, between articulation and mutism, between freedom and submission, within this narrow space on the cusp of repetitious blocks of housing. Le Corbusier's Unité in Firminy also potentially creates large or small transitional spaces/ elements that, acting as threshold, give character to and mediate between the individual and the collective. In the suburbs, so aptly named by Bellil as a world of "all or nothing", creating nuanced spaces that allow for adjusting one's ability to take a distance at times and join the crowd at will at other times will contribute to the possible distanciation Begag hypothesizes. Inserting liminal prompts creates a framework of action for design disciplines at various scales: Whether this is happening at the scale of the individual unit, at the scale of the ensemble or some units or an ensemble, at the scale of an entire cité or a constellation of a few of them, the insertion of spatial prompts might prove to be an appropriate strategy through which one can gradually foster change in such vulnerable terrain.

ENDNOTES

1 This paper is a small fragment of a larger ongoing research on the subject of HLM living entitled: *Rising measures*.

2 HLM stands for *habitation à loyer modéré* and is the common term for social housing or subsidized housing in France. The term Cités HLM refers to areas in which a large number of these housing projects are gathered often at the outskirts of urban areas.

3 Ronai, Simon, "Paris et la Banlieue: Je t'aime, moi non plus", *Hérodote, revue de géographie et de géopolitique*, second trimester, 2004. p. 28

4 *B13* or *Banlieue 13*, known in English as *District 13* is a movie, directed by Pierre Morel and produced by Luc Besson in 2004. The sequel was made in 2009, entitled: *Banlieue 13- Ultimatum*.

5 Begag, Azouz, *Les Dérouilleurs: ces Français de banlieue qui ont reussi, Paris : Mille et une nuits*, 2002

6 Begag states that those who were able to move out temporarily or distance themselves from the age of 13-17, for reasons related to school seems to have had a chance to consider different environments for a short period, which in turn becomes the precursor for moves later on. Ibid. p. 62.

7 Bellil, Samira, *To Hell and Back: The life of Samira Bellil,* translated by Lucy R. McNair; Introduction by Alec G. Hargreaves, Lincoln: University of Nebraska Press, c2008. While Bellil's support of certain women group might have caused some tensions between the people of the left and right in politics, her story remains deeply moving.

8 Ibid. p. 1. Samira passed away at the age of 31 in 2004 of stomach cancer.

9 Ibid. p. 30

10 Ibid. p. 30-31, Here Bellil asks the question of us, and of herself, recognizing the environment that surrounding her as the quintessential cause of her later problems. While she names other factors in her narrative (family, personal relationships, etc.) and knowing that ordeal that she suffered was a sum total of many different factors, the weight of the role of environment looms large in her qualification of misfortunes.

11 Ibid. p. 33.

12 Ibid. p. 34

13 We can see that Begag's claim on the weight of the *banlieue* as a consuming force, an omnipresence casting a continuous shadow on the life of its inhabitants is real and representative of feelings of some of the people who live in these neighborhoods. However to remedy issues of immigration, of inequality, racism, multiple phobias, cultural differences, etc. of the large population that inhabits the banlieues cannot be summed up in evacuating the HLMs at once.

14 Look at the Kechiche mention of his efforts for finding the "right"language, as well as that pdf paper.

15 L'Unité in Firminy became a co-op in 2003, the north portion reopened, and some of the units became larger by joining adjacent apartments together

16 The school project was under done under the supervision of Prof. Jean-Loup Hérbert, himself a resident of Unité.

17 Currently the upper floor of the Unite is housing a module of "cultural landscape studies" of Saint-Etienne University

46   Development of alluvial surface.
Harold Fisk for the Mississippi River Commission, 1943, Baton Rouge

PRESERVING THE FLOW

NATURAL DISASTER IN IGNORANCE

by JORG SIEWEKE

How can we advance recent ecological concepts from a human-centric towards an eco-centric perspective without wandering off into the spiritual world? Ecological concepts have been evolving as we learn to appreciate an eco-centric perspective embracing change beyond the concept of equilibrium.

The comparatively recent history of modernization and its effects become tangible if one faces the regulation of rivers. The juxtaposition of the vivid nature of the water relative to built structure intuitively reveals the project's implicit mindset of control and order. How can we begin to address the subdued animate nature of a river today?

How can we begin to understand what is " playing out " in southern Louisiana? How can we comprehend the inevitable drama of the lower Mississsippi, aka "Old Man River", an ecological disaster that may soon be followed by an economic disaster to then be misnamed a natural disaster.

Delta landscapes are among the most productive ecosystems of all: in terms of productivity they exceed tropical rainforests. Their rich metabolism provides an abundance of seafood as well as the most fertile agricultural land in the floodplains. The typical deltaic metabolism provides and maintains structures for ecosystems to thrive.

At the same time, this landscape of abundance is ephemeral. It does not remain stable in its local place for long, so nothing can be considered permanent except change itself as a defining parameter. The River will always alter its course, yet it will remain in the alluvial delta-fan. In Louisiana this principle was understood by the Native Americans, who adapted to the swampy ground with light and mobile forms of settlement on the natural levees or with subtle elevations such as heaps of oyster-shells.

Since the aftermath of the 1927 flood, the management of the Mississippi River and Tributaries Project (MRTP) has regulated the surrounding environment along a paradigm focused on averting change. The side effects of this regulation have now been acknowledged as quite significant, as the entire project's integrity is being questioned. Formerly marginalized externalities of channelizing the River surface have emerged today as unintended consequences at the scale of the entire project. A range of problems have developed, notably a) the loss of the Louisiana Delta landscape due to wetland erosion, b) an increased exposure of New Orleans to storm surge due to loss of deltaic cypress forest buffer, c) growing hypoxia dead zones of algae bloom along the Gulf Coast due to excess nutrient discharged by the River and d) the risk of loosing the youngest part of the MRTP itself, the Rivers navigable pass in the Bird-Foot Delta

The hinge point of the Delta fan is located at the confluence with the Red River; here the Mississippi would prefer to jump channels to a shorter and steeper path to the gulf. If it were for the River to decide, it would divert westwards into a lush cypress forest basin known as the Atchafalaya. The Mississippi River is tired of flowing past New Orleans; it has gone this way for too long. The sediment has elevated its own bed, and its levees have become the highest ground in the Delta. The River would rather follow gravity again and wander all around the Southern Louisiana Delta, building the most fertile land of sediment and nutrient by breaking through a levee occasionally. It would also want to push back the Gulf's salinity gradient of encroaching brackish water with its own volume of freshwater.

The nascent ambition of the River to shift had not been accounted for – quite the opposite. It has been conceptualized in static fashion as fixed in place, needing to accommodate industry and settlement. Great quantities of steel and concrete structural engineering have been brought in to turn the River's stability into stagnation. In the meantime, global trade and commerce of national and international reach rely on the river to stay where it is. In fact, a United States Congressional decision set in place since the 1950s prescribes not only its delineation, but the flow rate of the Mississippi as fixed to 70/30 in an attempt to prevent the river from following the entropic path into the Atchafalaya. All multi-faceted investment, reinsurance networks and economic tangents at stake require the stream to be

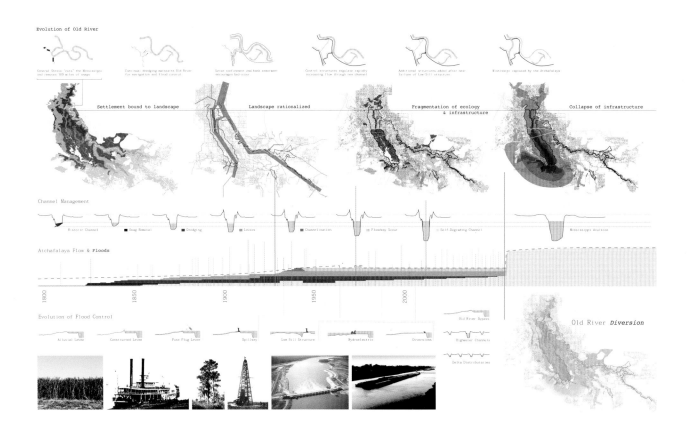

**ParadoXcity_Mapping Atchafalaya: Mississippi
Delta and Old River Control 2011**

reduced to a channel - a plumbing system or a discharge problem to use the current terminology of its managers.

As one consequence of channeling the adjacent Louisiana Delta is starving from being cut off from further sediment replenishment as the land erodes into the sea at increasing rates. The land subsides faster since the River is no longer allowed to supply its sediment deposit over the levees into the delta landscape. Instead, the accumulating sediment in the river clogs the shipping channel. Dredging the River for navigation can barely keep up today and will not be able to accommodate post-Panama class shipping drafts. Excess nutrients from agricultural run-off throughout the Mississippi watershed channeled to the Gulf is creating algae blooms. The decomposition of algae by bacteria consumes large amounts of oxygen and leaves barely any for other creatures. The Dead Zone in the Gulf of Mexico is turning an increasing area of the coast along the continental shelf into an oxygen-depleted Hypoxia Zone.

The Mississippi carries numerous neglected properties. The River's hydrologic regime, its sediment regime and its salinity regime, to name a few, have either been overlooked or knowingly marginalized in favor of mandating the Mississippi river as a shipping channel. The late consequences of this denial surface today in a scale that exceeds human control by far. The entire "plumbing project" commissioned by priorities of flood protection and navigation and shipping will no longer be able to provide for either of the two purposes. The project begins to bite its own tail.

The Lower Mississippi River and Tributary Project (MRTP) fails at precisely the scale of its misconduct with economical implications going far beyond it. The

potential loss of the Delta, as well as the MRTP itself, may threaten the city of New Orleans and the Port of Southern Louisiana. Consequently we ultimately arrive at the most basic question: What would the river do?

Despite the trillion dollars spent to avert change, the River will not be tamed. We therefore may need to reconsider our paradigm in facing intrinsic principles of change in landscapes, relative to the mandates projected on managing the river. How can we better understand landscape change and the intrinsic patterns of resiliency and adaptations to be smarter in making civilized infrastructures that better fit with riverscapes?

Alternative concepts for managing the Mississippi have been suggested in the past, as John Barry lays out descending voices in his epic narrative *Rising Tide*. More recently, a 1987 EPA study suggests that, instead of forcing the River and the Delta to freeze in its 1953 flow rate of 30/70 between the Atchafalaya and the Mississippi, a pro-active strategy would assume to collaborate with the River's dynamic trajectory and the deltaic transition. The next inevitable shift of the River would be guided in a gradual and controlled fashion utilizing the "Old River Control Structure" to avoid increased risk of catastrophic failure. The flow towards the Atchafalaya would be shifting at a rate of one percent a year, allowing the ecosystem and the economy to accommodate the transition incrementally. (EPA 1987 p. 42-41)

Preserving the flow
Measures taken to regulate the environment have assumed a state of stability but must more accurately be addressed as homeostasis or stationary stability. In contrast, most riverine regimes and ecosystems are more accurately characterized by the principle of homeorhesis

Installation of Revetments along the Mississippi
River banks by the Army Corp of Engineers

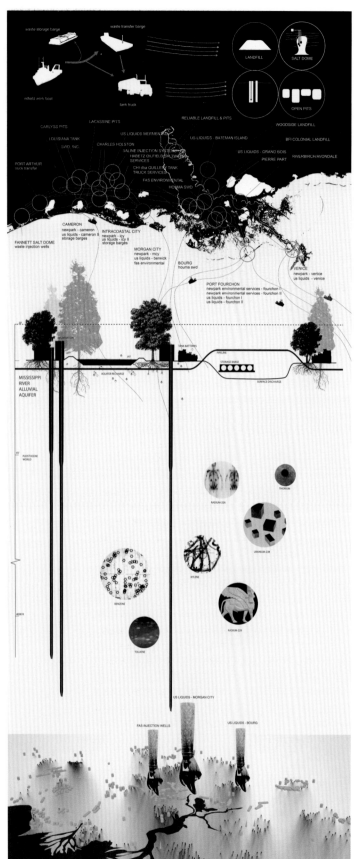

or evolutionary stability, a preservation of a system's characteristic flow processes (Waddington 1955).

Ecologists since Holling (1973) have expanded the notion of non-equilibrium ecosystems to the concept of resilience: a system's capacity to absorb changes and to persist in a globally stable dynamic regime far from equilibrium. Waddington expanded the concept of resilience building on catastrophe theory emerging at the time. He argues that every system is potentially moving towards moments of bifurcation where irreversible change occurs "catastrophically".

He applied catastrophe theory to multi-factorial development in biological morphogenesis. Waddington used topological 3D models of attractor surfaces occupied by the innumerous variables simultaneously altering these dynamic processes. His surface models are represented as folded planes indicating paths for an imagined sphere to follow, *aka chreod* (Greek for necessary path). In their topologic quality they appear very similar to a basic delta fan condition showing multiple distributary pathways. The points of bifurcation result from altering pushing and pulling variables in the surface, creating an epigenetic landscape. This concept assumes both a producing and a produced condition represented in the same surface.

If we translate the topological principle of folded surface into a delta fan landscape we would think of the bifurcations as distributaries or crevasses (natural diversions). The beauty of Waddington's epigenetic surface interpreted for the delta analogy is that, instead of running one pass through this model, we would think of the deltaic fan running multiple iterations until eventually the next necessary shifting occurs as an outcome of the River's own alteration to the system, namely the River silting up its bed, natural levee building and barrier island formations. The layered geological survey provides evidence of this pattern.

Waddington developed this topological diagram of an epigenetic landscape to communicate embryonic development studies. Although he did utilize the topological surface model to visualize his theory, he had no actual interest in rendering landscapes. Paradoxically in doing so he provides the meaningful abstraction of deltaic environment as a topology and the contingencies that are carried in it.

The ParadoXcity research on DeltaCities becomes instructive since deltas are by definition reassembled by ongoing dynamic geomorphological processes. As in a petri dish one may perceive ecosystem change in real time. Another emblematic condition of deltaic environments is the river as an identifiable driver of change. The rivers in pre-modern times were referred to as a subject or a god like entity. In the process of the secularization of nature that has occurred in modernity the river has been reduced to an object. Today we struggle with concepts to reassign animate qualities or agency to the river.

ParadoXcity_ Mapping Atchafalaya
Petrochemical Atchafalaya: contaminant storage facilities

PROPOSED

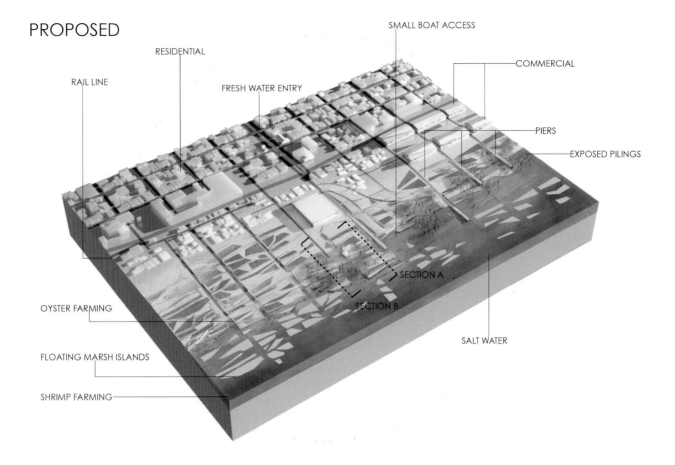

- SMALL BOAT ACCESS
- RESIDENTIAL
- RAIL LINE
- FRESH WATER ENTRY
- COMMERCIAL
- PIERS
- EXPOSED PILINGS
- SECTION A
- SECTION B
- OYSTER FARMING
- SALT WATER
- FLOATING MARSH ISLANDS
- SHRIMP FARMING

One starting point is to address nature not as a passive product (natura naturata) but as a producing entity (natura naturans). The appreciation of nature's self-organizing capacities allows understanding our role in facilitating a co-evolutionary path. The close reading of the animate and productive capacities also carry the potential of co-productivity. In contrast to the tradition of bio-mimicry (learning from natural form), we need to learn how to better understand natural systems' performance and organization and, most significantly, their metabolism. Bio-mimicry should therefore move from the objective of drawing from formal repertoire to a model for constructing and maintaining metabolic structures.

Instead of increasing measures of control by installing more grey infrastructure, how can we begin to appreciate how the deltaic metabolism provides structure for itself? Can we find ways to tap into these metabolic services without compromising their integrity with counterproductive infrastructure? The more recent interest in ecosystem services and green infrastructure can be understood as first attempts to identify the enduring or redundant productive capacities of "natural" systems.

These insights require a holistic perspective that apprehends the layered ecological amalgam's implications

and appreciates the culture/nature hybrids that reside in the swampy ground of deltas. (Jonas 2012)

In order to fully reconcile these alienated and unresolved nature/culture hybrids, we need to learn about contemporary critical ecosystem theory just as much as emerging discourse in the humanities that readjust our relationship to objects known as "object orientated philosophy."

We may begin to consider the river as a legal subject (Serres, 1995), as human/nonhuman hybrids (Latour, 1993) we created for ourselves and ultimately as something too large to fully comprehend and manage in its entity: a HyperObject (Morton 2013)

We need to focus on matters of concern of non-human entities. It's a call to disclose all the non-represented objects we have created ourselves and invite them to the Parliament of things. (Latour 1993)

In ecological terms co-evolution offers a path that accounts for both the human-centric perspective of landscapes' utility and the eco-centric perspective of landscapes' agency to identify synergies between the two.

Re-use of Tower House at Gortnaclea, County Laois

REMAPPING THE MIDLANDS

by JEFFREY BOLHUIS & LAURENCE LORD
IN COLLABORATION WITH MIRIAM DELANEY

Context

ReMapping the Midlands is a research-by-design project that focuses on the central region of the Republic of Ireland, commonly known as The Midlands. This is a predominately rural area characterised by its flat agricultural landscape dotted with towns and villages. Due to its lack of larger towns and understated natural beauty this area has traditionally been an overlooked and undervalued part of Ireland, often serving merely as a thoroughfare between the capital and economic centre of Dublin and the scenic destinations on the south and west coasts. It is an area that is passed through on the way to elsewhere. In recent years the economic dependency and transitional nature of the Midlands has been heightened by several crucial developments.

During the economic boom of the Celtic Tiger the Midlands became an attractive and more affordable housing location for people working in Dublin. The Dublin commuter belt extended far into the region and led to the expansion of existing towns and the construction of a large number of housing estates. The resulting increase in population in the Midlands was the highest in the country.[1] These new inhabitants, however, mostly valued the Midlands for its proximity to Dublin and not for its inherent qualities.

The subsequent economic downturn and housing crisis have led to a decrease in the desirability of the Midlands as a place to live. The global economic crisis has severely affected the fiscal situation of the country and the region in particular, which has led to a large surplus of devalued and unused housing and building stock. The relatively large negative effect of the economic shift on the Midlands is illustrated by the fact that unemployment among mortgage holders in this area is the highest in the country.[2]

Furthermore, new infrastructure has dramatically altered the experience and position of the region. Recently constructed motorways cut through the Midlands and bypass most of its towns, allowing travelers to traverse the entire area without interruption, further increasing its transitory nature.

As part of the nature of the region as a thoroughfare and its lack of strong identity or perceived qualities, the Midlands currently does not significantly benefit from the tourism potential in Ireland. The region falls substantially behind neighboring counties in terms of visitors per annum,[3] and the largest part of the region is not promoted by Failte Ireland.[4]

Site.
The project established an area of focus defined by several infrastructural and natural boundaries with the River Shannon to the west, the meeting of the Grand Canal and the Barrow Waterway to the east, the M4 motorway to the north and the M6 and M7 to the south.

Technically the Midland region encompasses only the counties of Laois, Offaly, Longford and Westmeath; it was decided, however, to apply the term loosely to a region and not follow any key political boundary lines. It is the intention that this project can eventually extend into or be linked to areas outside of our initial site. There is no hard line edge to the project area; it is merely our area of focus. The boundary can be expanded and contracted to incorporate further fields of study if required. The study area therefore also incorporates parts of the counties of Roscommon, Westmeath, Meath, Galway, Offaly, Kildare, Tipperary, Laois and Kilkenny.

Within this defined area the authors have selected medium sized towns that have been most affected by the recent motorway bypasses and economic decline. (Moate, Kilbeggan, Rochfortbridge and Enfield along the N4 and N6, Monasterevin, Mountrath and Borris-in-Ossory along the N7 and Abbeyleix and Durrow along the old N8.) These towns are large enough to sustain communities and some services but too small to function as independent economic entities. The selected towns all have a population between 500 and 3000 and were originally situated on the main thoroughfares, but subsequently bypassed by the new motorways.[5]

Issues.
As a result of the twin forces of economic decline and their new status as bypassed towns, the towns within the study area face an uncertain future. To a large extent the towns had become economically dependent on the trade generated from the high volume of passing traffic. For this reason the newly constructed motorway bypasses have had a severe detrimental impact on the towns in terms of both economy and activity: petrol stations have closed and most hotels, restaurants and pubs in the region have suffered loss in business.

Many towns also underwent rapid expansion as commuter towns and due to the housing crisis are now left with a large stock of uninhabited or disused houses and buildings. Many of the 'ghost estates' of Ireland can be found here. These are housing estates, which had been constructed during the economic boom and are now (partially) unfinished or uninhabited.[6] These incomplete developments serve as a stark reminder of the inflated Irish property market of the early part of this century. Currently the long process of exorcising these 'ghost estates' is starting to begin, with the resolution for some of the more hopeless cases being the bulldozer.

Defined for so long by their position on major national routes, the towns are now struggling to deal with their new condition. These towns are ripe for re-definition.

Potential.
Despite the negative impacts of the bypasses there is also a positive side: with the loss of the large volume of noisy and polluting traffic, some of the wide streets of these market towns are freed up. Even though the towns in the area have been cut of from the major routes, many are still easily accessible from Dublin. Their proximity makes them ideally suited as destinations for day trips from the capital.

The new infrastructure of motorways also provides the region with an even better connection to all the other regions in Ireland. The area of study can be reached in 1-3 hours by car from the cities of Dublin, Limerick and Galway and 1-2 hours by train. All major airports in the country can be reached within 1-3 hours. This provides the region with large potential in terms of national and international visitors. In terms of accessibility within the region, the Midlands possess a very dense network of partially disused/underused infrastructure of roads, railways and canals. Combined with the largely flat terrain these provide the landscape the potential of being very easily accessible by a large variety of transportation methods including bicycles, canoes and kayaks.

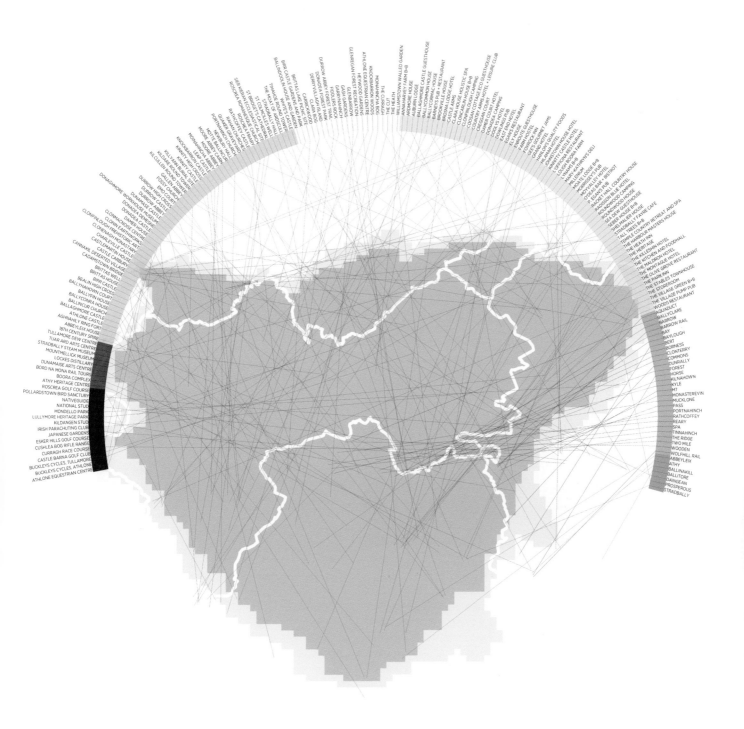

Despite the current relatively low regard of the Midlands in terms of tourism, there is in fact an over abundance of potential for (alternative) tourism within the region. The bypassed towns are all situated near several excellent amenities and points of interest many of which are overlooked and underused: cutaway bogs, canals and waterways, countless historical ruins, forests, mountains, rivers and gardens.

Strategy.

Up to this point these towns and the counties within the study area have been working in isolation to promote their own interests. There is a lack of regional strategy, which would benefit the Midlands as a whole. This study therefore aims to define an overall strategy for the region that overcomes county borders and jurisdictions. It is a strategy that aims to reinforce the undervalued

As a backbone of the strategy, the study proposes a network consisting of an alternative infrastructure that will form the basis of the re-development of the by-passed towns and the entire region. This will link these towns back into the region by making them the nodes in the new network.

The network between these towns will also connect all points of interest in the area and provide a new framework for community and tourism needs. The alternative infrastructure will provide a social amenity and will also act as an attractor and a new identity for the area, thereby becoming a generator for tourism and further benefitting the existing communities.

The underutilized service facilities, which previously provided for the roads (petrol stations, cafes and restaurants) as well as former industrial sites (disused buildings and structures) will be adapted and reintegrated as facilities along the new tourism routes. New industries and ventures could be developed as part of this successful network.

One example could be the introduction of a regional version of the hugely successful Dublin shared bikes scheme[7] where bicycles can be picked up and dropped off at the towns, allowing both local inhabitants as well as tourists to enjoy the network at a minimal cost. Furthermore a variety of eco-tourism and cottage industries can be developed from the existing agriculture infrastructure along the network, and local amenities can be improved.

Once established, this network will function as an attractor and provide a new identity to the area. On a national scale it will offer an interesting and quieter alternative to the highly visited areas in the surrounding regions, and so attract a new type of tourist to the region and Ireland.

[Re] Map.

A key part of the study was analyzing the site from several sources and new maps were drawn in order to determine the location of existing amenities and infrastructure and their potential merits for the new network.

A striking feature within the area is the over supply of secondary roads as a result of the agrarian practice of inter-generational land division.[8] Due to their scale and meandering lines and diverse character, as a result of following medieval property lines and topography, these roads are in fact ideally suited for low speed traffic such as cycling and horse riding. Several key railways traverse the region, primarily going from Dublin to the west and south. Railway lines ending in Ballina, Westport, Galway, Limerick and Cork pass through the site with the major local train stations being Athlone, Tullamore and Portlaoise. However, for the new network these hubs would serve as gateway points. Of particular interest are the disused railways and the soon to be post-industrial railways. The Midlands have historically been central to

qualities in the region by making better use of the existing towns, infrastructure, landscape and amenities.

An important principle of the strategy is to not add or build where it is not necessary but only re-use what already exists. This allows the project to focus on utilizing the enormous latent potential that is already present in the Midlands. The authors believe that with a minimal amount of financial investment and a creative use of the existing structures and regional qualities, a new identity can be forged that adds value to the entire region.

The new bypassed condition of the towns provides them an opportunity to take on a new identity, re-connecting them to their rich surroundings and in doing so re-defining them as destinations in their own right. This will allow the communities to be less dependent on the larger cities and reconnect them to their landscapes and topographical hinterlands. Within the towns themselves the high street, no longer a miniature motorway, can once again become the core of the community.

TOP
Industrial Railway re-used as horse riding, cycling and foot path

BOTTOM
New bridge across Grand Canal Lock near Edenderry, County Offaly

Bord na Móna, a semi state Irish company responsible for the harvesting of peat, and their involvement in the industrial turf extraction. Due to the depletion of peat stocks, however, a wealth of disused industrial railways are being left behind that could be adapted and re-used as part of the eco-infrastructure network.

Both the Grand Canal and the Royal Canal traverse the site, with the Barrow Waterway emerging from the South. These 18th century waterway networks have fallen into disrepair since the 1970's, but recently there has been significant development in promoting these, in particular the New Triangle, which links the Royal Canal, the Shannon Waterway and the Grand Canal. Many of the key government bodies associated with waterway infrastructure such as Discover Ireland, Waterways Ireland and the Inland Waterway Association of Ireland (IWAI) are currently championing this.[9]

Several tourist, historic and cycling routes are also within the study area, some of which are confined to a specific county, such as the Westmeath and the Offaly way. Others are the Mullingar Cycle route and the intriguing Gordon Bennett Route,[10] an historical car race route from 1903 that is still celebrated with classic car runs. These are established routeways, most with clearly marked wayfinding and signage. However, all these routes are independent and as yet there has not been any initiative that connects these to form a larger network.

Finally all points of interest were mapped. There many points of natural beauty, such as the Slieve Bloom mountains, the Boora complex and Donadea forest park. A multitude of important historical sites are located in the area such as Clonmacnoise, Dunamase, Emo Court and Durrow High Cross. Other notable points of interest are the Heywood gardens, the Japanese Gardens, the National Stud, Stradbally Steam Museum and the Bord na Mona Rail Tours. As part of the inventory activity centres, hotels, restaurants and pubs of particular interest were included.

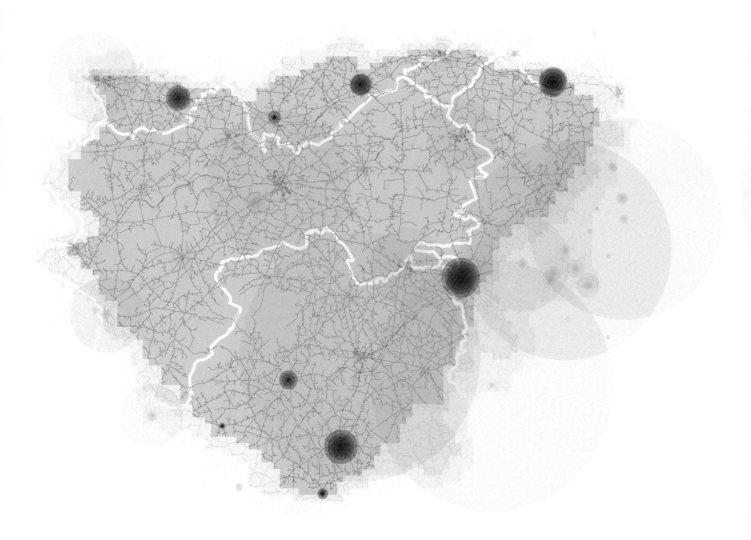

Relative Urban population nodes throughout site (Rings in increments of 500 people)

Network.

The proposed new transportation network will use existing infrastructure and form an alternative to the main road network. It will directly link the previously bypassed towns and connect them to the most important points of interest in the area. The scaffold of the network will be a portion of the secondary roads, selected according to their scenery and suitability for cycling or walking. The routes these roads form are determined by their logic of connecting the towns and points of interest in the area. In order to establish these links, the intensity of the points of interest was determined by placing a km grid over the site.

The network will furthermore incorporate the waterways, abandoned or post industrial railroads and existing routeways in the area. This network will so serve as a new type of slower more pleasant eco-infrastructure. It will allow people to traverse the entire region and visit the points of interest as well as all the bypassed towns. It will not only provide the disjointed communities of these bypassed towns with a shared public facility but will also help generate a new industry of eco-tourism. It is the aim that in time this network will become the catalyst for a series of new industries.

The very diverse nature of the new transportation system demands a clear branding and advertising in order to establish the basis of a new identity for the region. The study incorporates proposals for architectural interventions located at key sites along the route.

These add to or make use of existing structures and will enhance the identity of the network as well as providing important amenities. Furthermore, interactive applications and websites will be developed as part of the network. These platforms will provide information and allow users to add content to create an ever-increasing database of the network.

[Re] Use.

Part of the proposed strategy is to improve and amplify the access and experience of the new network by series of interventions that make use of existing structures. There is an abundance of underused building stock across the country, particularly in the Midlands, and the study proposes sustainable ways of re-using some this potential.

An example of this is the many petrol stations that now lie unused; these could become bicycle rental locations and café pit stops. Tying in with these same cycle routes, another key feature that would be adapted and re-used as part of the network is the industrial railways. This infrastructure offers huge potential to be re-used as a new network for cycle routes or walk ways.

Adapting the principle of the Norwegian Nasjonale Turistveger,[11] pavilions could be located at key points along the network to serve as facilities and destinations in their own right. Small pavilions, correctly located, to offer shelter, frame views and offer facilities could hugely benefit the definition and attraction of the net-

Slieve Bloom viewing point, County Laois

work. The Midlands, just as the rest of Ireland, is blessed with many locations of natural beauty and viewpoints that should be utilized to their full potential to help to accentuate the inherent scenic value of the area. As the Midlands finds it beauty in subtle landscapes this can be achieved through understated and high quality architectural interventions.

Within the context of this study, the most suitable locations for the first of these interventions are the Slieve Bloom Mountains and the Grand Canal.

Similarly the wealth of historical artifacts should also be utilized. For example, a series of tower house ruins are spread across the area. Small additions would provide these beautiful Irish structures with a new use and a potential source of income. As part of this project we have made a study of the forgotten tower house at Gortnaclea, County Laois, less than a kilometre away from the new N7 motorway. This would be a perfect location for a viewing platform that could be inserted without damaging the existing ruin.

Conclusion.

The economic crisis and bursting of the housing bubble along with recent large infrastructural changes have all contributed to the significant problems for the Midlands. Nevertheless, we feel that the current condition provides a unique opportunity to re-assess the quality of the area, which could lead to improvements in terms of economy, livability and community. We propose to add value by re-evaluating. With this study we have developed a strategy for the potential re-development of the Midlands that uses its inherent qualities and moribund infrastructure to establish a stronger identity.

By mapping, analyzing and re-evaluating the current condition we are able to propose strategic interventions and adaptations that often require a minimal financial and material input in order to realize a significant positive effect. Through the creation of an alternative infrastructure and eco-tourism network the region is able to reposition itself in terms of its identity and what it can offer to the local communities and potential visitors. This network can then also form the basis of a series of projects and industries and create a common identity for the region that consists of counties and towns that are too small to individually initiate a holistic strategy of this scale.

The proposed adaptive re-use of historic sites serves as best practice of our overall strategy of re-use instead of new build, which is driven by the crisis. It also creates unique opportunities and offers a positive outlook on the questions raised by historic ruins and the recent ghost estates.

Although this study is focused on a specific context the ideas behind the strategy for ReMapping the Midlands will also have merit to other areas. Currently there seems to be an increasing desire for community

based and local initiatives that mitigate the negative effects and anxiety caused by the economic crisis and continuing globalization. In this way the idea of creating a localised physical network based on specific qualities of region is a principle that can bring value to many regions.

Although the current economic climate forces us as designers to work with minimal means, we believe that we are not also forced to minimize our goals. Through carefully assessing the quality of what is already present and how this can be used, combined or adapted, we are able to accomplish a macro effect in a more pleasing and sustainable manner. It is precisely in this strategic thinking that our strength as a profession lies and how we, as architects and urban planners, can best contribute to the current discourse.

ENDNOTES

1 "Irish Census studies 2006-2011" www.cso.ie/en/census/Census2011PreliminaryReport/ Relative increase in population based on CSO.ie report from Central Statistics Office, Ireland.

2 "Irish Census studies 2006-2011" www.cso.ie/en/census/Census2011PreliminaryReport/ Unemployment among mortgage holders based on CSO.ie report from Central Statistics Office, Ireland.

3 "Policy and Futures, Failte Ireland" www.failteireland.ie Irish Tourist Board information from the published statistics from the period of 2009-2011 in terms of tourist visits per region.

4 www.failteireland.ie Irish Tourist Board information based on the counties currently promoted on international website.

5 "A Decade of Progress" National Roads Authority, Ireland www.nra.ie/public-private-partnership/a-decade-of-progress/

6 "621 'ghost estates' built across State" Pope, Conor The Irish Times. 30 April 2010.

7 "What's the secret of the Dublin bike hire scheme's success?" Daly, Maria www.theguardian.com/environment/bikeblog/2011/aug/04/dublin-bike-hire-scheme

8 A History of Irish Farming, 1750-1950 Bell, Jonathan and Watson, Mervyn October, 2011

9 "Lakelands & Inland Waterways Strategic Plan 2010–2015" Waterways of Ireland www.waterwaysireland.org

10 "Gordon Bennett Route" Grand Tour: Touring Routes Ireland www.grandtour.ie/tour/gordon-bennett-route/

11 "Scenic Roads for exploring Norway's breathtaking landscapes" National Tourist Routes in Norway www.nasjonaleturist-veger.no.en

LESSONS FROM QUEENSLAND FOR VIABLE FUTURES

RESILIENCE, ADAPTABILITY, SUSTAIN-ABILITY AND RELATIONALITY

by NAOMI HAY AND TONY FRY

Australia is one of the Climate Change front line nations. As the driest inhabited continent on earth, much of Australia's climate is notoriously erratic and heavily influenced by ocean currents. Within a single year, in a single region, there can be an experience of drought, devastating fires, cyclones and floods. And there can be little doubt that the continuing cycle of warming of the planet has served to accelerate these already unstable conditions. The summer of 2012/13 was Australia's hottest in recorded history with average temperatures broken right across the spectrum.[1] As one of the world's wealthiest nations, can it cope with this emergent situation? And if it cannot cope, what are the implications for poorer nations? And where do approaches to adaptability and resilience fit within this context? Our starting point is to look at the climate events in the state of Queensland over the past three years.

What's with the weather?

Queensland, with a population of close to 4.7 million people, is Australia's second largest state, spanning over 1.7 million square kilometres.[2] The state is crossed by the Tropic of Capricorn and due to its vastness, encompasses a range of climatic and topographic variations. It combines everything from long sandy beaches and islands, high country, agricultural plains and sub-tropical rainforests to the Great Barrier Reef in the north. Its coastal strip and low lying river plains are subject to rapid onset flooding, from northern monsoonal rains in summer to heavy precipitation low pressure systems in spring and autumn. Summers are hot and humid; winters are dry, particularly in the north. Queensland, along with the rest of the country, is highly urbanised along its coastline.[3]

The Great Dividing Range separates the coastline from the wide expanse of agricultural belts, which are hotter and drier than the coastline. Here, inland rivers are slow moving, winding across vast flat plains, and in the wet season floodwaters may sit for weeks or even months across wide expanses of country. And beyond the productive agricultural plains lie the hot interior deserts. Rainfall throughout the state fluctuates considerably from decade to decade, region to region.[4]

Queensland then is highly accustomed to extreme weather. But the summer of 2010/11 delivered a series of weather events that caught all the state's residents, businesses, industries and governments by surprise. After one of the wettest years on record, the remains of an ex-tropical cyclone combined with an extensive La Nina weather pattern, dumping heavy rains. This

Places where the trouble starts: Two and a half years after half sections mountain road were washed away, works are underway.

resulted in dispersed flooding throughout an already saturated state. A further massive and slow-moving monsoonal trough then crossed the coast in the lead up to Christmas, creating an exceptional rain event culminating in destructive flooding which wreaked unprecedented damage across the length of the state, tragic loss of life and a damage bill of multi billions of dollars. The capital Brisbane, a city with a population of 1.8 million people, experienced its worst flood event in close to four decades.[5] It is estimated that by the end of that summer, more than 200,000 people were affected and 35 lives were lost as a result.[6]

With the majority of Queensland still in clean up and reconstruction mode, February 2011 saw severe Tropical Cyclone Yasi cross the coast, flattening the northern communities of Mission Beach and Tully, with a combination of coastal storm surges, extreme wind destruction and heavy rain once again leaving behind extensive flooding in the northern river catchments. There was little reprieve for the remainder of 2011 and early 2012,

Places where the trouble starts: Ten kilometres up the road rebuilding a forty-metre deep road washout is finished.

with further extended rain events bringing widespread repeated flooding to communities throughout the south-west and south-east of the state. Then, less than a year later in January 2013, the after effects of yet another cyclone once again produced extensive riverine flooding and damage to communities state-wide, many of those still struggling with the onerous recovery process from the disasters of 2011.

Many Communities across Queensland have been hit relentlessly, including regional centres such as Gympie (flooding five times in three years) and Bundaberg (which experienced severe flooding in 2010/11, to be followed with another flood that destroyed a significant section of the city only two years later). [7,8] Counting the financial costs, the Queensland State Government estimates that damage from these natural disasters to infrastructure alone has reached 2.1b, 7.1b, 2.1b and 2.5b to date in 2010, 2011, 2012 and 2013 respectively ($AU). [9] State and federal governments have responded reactively and predictably, launching an $80m 'Betterment Fund', aimed at 'strengthening resilience' of Queensland's critical infrastructure. [10] There can be little doubt, however, that the token funding is no more than a quick-fix, (non) solution to complex problems and critical issues of vulnerability brought into focus by '(un)natural' and often human induced disasters.

Historically, the majority of Queensland's urban settlements were situated on rivers, creeks and estuaries for the convenience of transportation. Population centres grew rapidly, ignoring the risks of life established upon low lying coastal floodplains. But now, they face the consequences of continually rebuilding homes and workplaces post extreme weather events. Riverine flooding results when watercourses lose their capacity to disperse high volumes of water during times of continuous heavy rainfall. Storm surges and high tides combine with these events, increasing their effects in coastal areas. In the flat inland agricultural plains of Queensland, riverine flooding is slow-rise, often covering thousands of square kilometers, frequently lasting for many months and isolating entire regions. [11]

In coastal Queensland, flash floods occur as a result of the intense sudden downpours from seasonal low pressure and monsoonal weather systems. Drainage systems in urban zones designed for average runoffs fail. This event occurs rapidly and unpredictably and poses significant threat to life and property. Again it results from a failure to appreciate risk, a lack of planning and foresight. Reducing the ability of the ground to absorb the rapid downpour of water by constructing hard surfaces makes the situation worse. It creates excessive urban runoff, thereby putting drainage systems under great pressure. Removing mangroves and vegetation along the soft sandy rivers and coastlines in the name of development also creates problems. [12] The foreshore destabilizes and erosion accelerates, altering the path and

form of natural watercourses. Inappropriate construction upon sites prone to water runoff, underspecified levy banks and, in the case of Brisbane, a dam not built for capacity in such extreme events all add to the risk of future disaster.

The floods in South East Queensland in January 2011 were a combination of all of the above. The city of Toowoomba and its surrounds, on the crest of the Great Dividing Range, experienced torrential rainfall on already soaked soil, which was swiftly channeled over hard surfaces and via altered water courses that converge in the cities central business district, resulting in a terrible flash flood which has since been described as an 'inland tsunami'. A further torrent of water rushed down the hills to the Lockyer Valley heading for Brisbane, en route destroying several small towns and their communities and overcharging the Brisbane River downstream. Meanwhile, the dam built for flood mitigation and Brisbane's water storage (already well above its storage capacity) had its floodgates opened. Residents in low lying areas (including both the old, and the newly established expanding subdivisions) of Ipswich and Brisbane were told to move to higher ground. Within 48 hours, both cities were inundated.

The immediate consequences - the loss of human life (of course, as a developed nation, these losses were dramatically less than our poorer regional neighbours experience) and the devastation of entire communities - were conveyed relentlessly through familiar media imagery. This, in the aftermath of the floods, included the visual imagery of the so called "Mud Army" comprising thousands of community volunteers, who arrived by the busload to help total strangers.

Queensland already maintains a large permanent volunteer State Emergency Service (SES) for events such as these. But even with the help of the Australian Army, it was soon realised that the sheer scale of the clean-up operation could not be dealt with by government and the SES alone. A call was put out by Brisbane's City Council for volunteers and the response was overwhelming. While more than 23,000 officially registered and lined up armed with shovels, gloves and gumboots for the clean-up, many, many more thousands rolled up their sleeves and helped family, friends and neighbours. Approximately 240,000 tons of water damaged furniture, equipment and filthy building waste were removed in the process. [13] Carpenters, electricians, plumbers, truck drivers and anyone who could wield a shovel or hose arrived from across the state, and many from interstate, to volunteer in any way they could. The enormity of this task, the self-less generosity of the volunteers and the level of both physical and emotional support offered served to lift the entire community's spirit in a time of need. Here was a snapshot of the larger community's willingness to unite and, in turn, to cope in their own way, with the aftermath of disaster. The scenes along the Brisbane River have been repeated around regional Queensland in the many flood events that have since occurred.

Queensland is still in a state of interminable rebuilding. Local economies have been devastated, with recovery of live-stock, crops, business and industry measured not in months, but over many years. Simultaneously land value has disintegrated in high-risk areas, leaving many families with little or no financial security and, as a result, no choice but to rebuild their existing vulnerable properties. Whilst the recovery of essential services and state owned assets including schools, roads, bridges, rail, airports and ferry terminals has been relatively swift in urban regions, in regional Queensland the work has been slower.

The Queensland State Government, unlike other state governments within Australia, does not maintain a reinsurance policy against disaster. Instead, reliance is upon a self-insurance policy coupled with an arrangement previously struck with the Federal Government to cover 75% of costs in the event of catastrophe.[14] As a consequence of the disasters of 2011, the Australian Government announced a flood levy in the form of additional income tax to be paid by all Australians in the following financial year, to help cover costs of essential infrastructure rebuilding.[15] The question remains, however, in the face of the prospect of an increasing number of extreme weather events, whether governments or the general public will be willing or able to cover the costs of perpetual rebuilding, or whether reinsurance options in the future will prove prohibitively expensive.

The 'Natural Disaster Insurance Review,' announced by the Australian Government to address issues of residential underinsurance, lacked clarity and did little to enable insurance affordability, except making a soft recommendation that residents in high risk areas be offered discounted insurance premiums through a government funded reinsurance scheme.[16] An extensive consultation process to consider such recommendations was announced.[17] But is it really feasible for governments to underwrite insurance for individuals in vulnerable locations on any long term basis? Moreover, the scale of the problem is too large and complex to be dealt with at such a limited level. It's likely that insurance issues will continue to be dealt with by the industry in their quest to maintain market competitiveness. However, the problems people living in vulnerable locations face go well beyond insurance. The question of what these problems are must now be addressed with urgency, as there is little doubt that global warming will increase the vulnerability of millions of people around the planet.

Climate change (both warming and cooling of the earth) pre-dates human existence and in the past had huge impacts upon it, but now the rapid acceleration of warming in recent years is amplifying our anthropocentric and unsustainable actions that both damage our ecologies of dependence and the viability of our own future. Although humanity has an inherent capacity for adaption (and has survived the multiple challenges of climate change over many thousands of years), large numbers of people living in expanding cities worldwide dramatically increases risk.[18,19] Adaptation in current circumstances demands a massive design effort, including infrastructure able to resist climatic impacts over one hundred years and more. Decisions about where and how people need to live, taking account of future risks, including floods, fires and coastal inundation, must become fundamental to the planning process.[20] The inability of global political policy to deal with global warming means the imperative to adapt becomes critically important.[21,22] Approaches to disaster in Queensland, in common with many other places, remain instrumental and largely technocentric, focusing upon rapid recovery and reconstruction. In contrast, reduction, mitigation and preparedness are neglected actions, while the cultural development of community resilience and adaptive capability is almost, if not totally, ignored.

Acting otherwise

The challenge for design professionals is to explore possibilities beyond traditional and pragmatic solutions: this by pre-empting and designing for future risk as an opportunity for redirective development strategy, as well as one that can build a culture of resilience and adaptability within communities seeking long-term sustainable futures in challenging times.

The resilience of a community is often characterised by two forms. Hard resilience refers to the strength of structures and institutions when placed under pressure, whereas soft resilience refers to the ability of a community to recover without fundamental changes to its structure and function.[23] Such thinking needs to be replaced by methods that are far more relational. The more resilient a community, the less vulnerable it becomes; a community that is truly resilient has the socio-cultural means and psychological strength to cope with change proactively as well as reactively, qualities essential in determining long term survival.[24] Vulnerability assessment and strategic planning strategies must be created out of the community and cooperatively designed with them so as to strengthen resolve and 'relational resilience' capability. This requires communities both gaining a detailed understanding of topography, planning, infrastructure, services and legal constraints, as well as a sound grasp of the natural and the artificial environments - together with the ability to examine existing socio-economic and political structures of communities – so they may be transformed to better cope with disaster.

Beyond such pragmatics, resilience and adaption is indivisible from the development of community within and by the community (not the same as officially

introduced 'community development'). This requires the formation of a dialogical process that moves from a general discussion on the future to how specific and different futures can be valued, created and sustained. Such action can be triggered by consideration of 'design in time' - that is: design in the medium of time combined with design urgency in the face of pressing problems. It also goes to the issue of learning from the past.

Community itself must be not only be the generator of future adaptive capacity and action, but it must also be enabled/enable itself to acquire a pre-emptive designed approach. This requires the creation of a process wherein appropriate design knowledge is developed in collaboration with appropriately informed design professionals willing and able to support the process. Such an approach needs a critical evaluation of all options, a willingness to explore new ideas and a recognition of the imperative of identifying and working with cultural difference of age, cultural attachment to place, change (modest and radical) and so on. Of particular concern is finding ways to adequately deal with questions of acting in the short term and purely instrumentally, as obstacles to establishing mid and long-term sustainable solutions.

More than this an openness to confront difficult yet essential questions is vital. Questions like: what must be designed, what must be eliminated, what can be adapted? Likewise, how can developers be stopped from building for expanding populations in vulnerable locations, constructing highly inappropriate built environments vulnerable to future risk, whilst being encouraged to work with communities to create safe and sustainable alternatives?

The designed approach presented here goes beyond retrofitting to embrace the creation of new built environments better able to deal with climate impacts combined with "metrofitting" existing cities at risk. Metrofitting is conceived as a co-ordinated approach beyond the limitations of retrofitting, whereby governments, policy makers, industry and individuals alike relationally co-ordinate responses that are preventative and adaptive across all levels of the socio-economic, the cultural, the constructed and the technical. Metrofitting acknowledges that which exists in a condition of structural unsustainability, addressing this in terms of adaptive capacity: to climate change, to population growth, to disaster, to displacement, to conflict, to social inequity, to politi-

Places where the trouble starts: Two and a half years after half sections mountain road were washed away, works are underway.

cal instability. It is the adaptive capacity of the social ecology of the city that is engaged and at stake here, not simply the restructuring of the built environment and its institutions.[25] Pre-figurative design for disassembly, modification, transportability, re-use, re-purposing, re-cycling and authentic extended lifecycles are just a few of the pre-emptive strategies that invite being embraced by professionals leading the way, including to far more ethical design practices. Stepping outside preconceived, aestheticized and technocentric agendas - embedded within the traditionally singular disciplinary practices of architecture, planning, interior and product - to rec-ognize the relational complexity of 'at risk' communities, their long term sustainable needs, and the establish-ment of social responsibility is essential.

Our population centres do not exist in a constant state of equilibrium; they are inherently transitional and must be recognized as such. Designing appropri-ate strategies for this continuous state of flux is vital to ensure future adaptive capabilities for all population centres. The urban as adaptable relies not just upon an appropriate and sustainable material fabric, infra-structure and a food producing natural environment. It also needs educational institutions with a curriculum focused upon long term adaptability and sustain-ability (including the utilization of local materials and crafts-manship, waste reduction and so on). But more than this it needs activities that bring people together to learn, share and care – the creation of these activities being of equal importance to seemingly more practical measures. The before mentioned actions of South East Queensland's Mud Army demonstrate a local willingness and capacity to engage as a larger community of care after a disaster has occurred. Bringing the community together as prefigurative action towards adaptation is the next essential step in the process.

The way forward

With the increasing effects of climate change now im-possible to ignore, Queensland cannot simply continue to throw good money after bad. Such quick-fix solutions in a never ending cycle of short term replacement will likely be unaffordable in the years to come. As some of the world's most financially privileged people, we have much to learn from some of the world's most undeveloped nations. The people of Bangladesh have enabled themselves to adapt accordingly to their own unfolding crisis. In a heavily populated and low lying country faced with severe annual monsoonal flooding, the effects of climate change are being faced head on by locals with low-tech solutions.[26] Here, farmers and villagers build embankments from soil and turf to hold back floodwaters and plant vegetation to ease erosion. With the help of volunteer organizations communities are lifting houses, protecting drinking water, planting vegetables on rooftops and raising simple flood shelter

zones for the protection of livestock, produce, posses-sions and people in times of flooding. All of this is made possible through a program of community education and training, under the guidance of local disaster pre-paredness committees.[27]

It is communities such as these, understanding the importance of prefigurative action and taking respon-sibility for their own futures, which are paving the way forward. Adaptability and resilience are being tackled from a bottoms-up perspective, with solutions that are practical, affordable and achievable within communities of little means.

There are some parallels that can be drawn here with Queensland since the 2010/11 floods in community

engagement and education (although obviously backed
with more substantial financial means). The Queensland
Government and the Local Government Association
of Queensland Community Development Engagement
Initiative has been initiated across seventeen local
councils. One such example is the 'Gympie Get Ready'
Resilience Program in which locals participate in
workshops learning skills in preparedness and disaster
management, resilience, emotional impact, adaptive
leadership and best practice community engagement.[28]
Similar resilience building projects have been developed
throughout Brisbane, Bundaberg and some of the worst
hit regional communities across the state.[29] Further
initiatives include Green Cross Australia's 'Harden

Up-Protecting Queensland' website, a comprehensive
database and community portal, providing information
on thousands of historical weather events, community
education, volunteering information, preparedness and
emergency service information and Disaster Connect,
a social media initiative providing the latest up to date
disaster information.[30]

But perhaps the most vivid example of community
adaptation in Queensland can be seen in the tiny town
of Grantham. With a population of only 360 people,
Grantham in the Lockyer Valley was one of the hardest
hit in the January 2011 flood. 120 of its homes were destroyed, damaged beyond repair or severely inundated
and many lives were tragically lost. An Australian first

Downriver where the ramifications are clear:

**Basements of the CBD containing substations, data servers and building
management systems filled with flood waters which took many months to
pump out, clean up and restore.**

land swap initiative was devised to move the town to higher ground, and to date 88 blocks of land have been swapped between community and council, with more pending. All residents in low lying areas of the valley were offered the opportunity to move to higher ground, with the local council acquiring a large land parcel that was flood free, but still maintaining close physical connection to the existing township. The exercise required an involved and intense community consultation process that resulted in a Master Plan being developed within four months of initiation.[31] The investment by council is estimated to be between 30m and 40m ($AU) and includes a new community centre, memorial parklands, show grounds and market place.[32]

Along with the new construction process, the town's historic Butter Factory, which had been in neglected disuse since the 1970's has now been handed back to the community by the Rotary Club of Toowoomba South. The building served as an emergency centre immediately after the floods, as a rescue point and storage facility for donated goods. The building though was in need of serious retrofitting, with concrete cancer and

asbestos linings to be dealt with and a replacement roof needed. But the historical and more importantly emotional connection of the building to what remained of the township was deemed too important to ignore. Restoration was made possible with larger community donations of 1.5 m in cash and another .5m($AU) in materials and kind. An estimated 3000 volunteer hours were donated to the project.[33] The Butter Factory now serves as a function centre, a gathering place and as recognition for a community that has rebuilt itself for a viable and resilient future.

What is being created here is the fabric of a care structure underpinning community, which is essential for adaptive capacity and long term viable futures. The design community and the people of Queensland can rise to these challenges by tackling issues of resilience, adaptability and long-term sustain-ability up-front, rather than waiting for the next crisis. The risks are predictable and can no longer be underestimated or ignored. The time to think and act beyond the immediate is now.

ENDNOTES

1 Will Steffan and Climate Commission, "The Angry Summer," Commonwealth of Australia Department of Climate Change and Energy Efficiency, 2013, 2, accessed November 25,2013, http://www. climatecommisssion.gov.au.

2 Queensland Government, "Queensland Population Counter," accessed November 25, 2`013, http://www.oesr.qld.gov.au/products/briefs/pop-growth-qld/qld-pop-counter.php.

3 Queensland Government, "Towns and Regions," accessed November 25, 2013, http://www.qld.gov.au/about/about-queensland/towns/general-info.

4 This variation is brought about by the El Nino Southern Oscillation (ENSO). When the surface temperature of the tropical Pacific Ocean is warm, an El Nino system brings fewer heavy rainfall events. Conversely, when the surface of the ocean is in a cooling phase a La Nina system accompanies wetter conditions, heavy rainfall and destructive cyclones. When combined with the slower cycle of ocean temperature variations known as the Interdecadal Pacific Oscillation, the result is a climate that fluctuates through periods of intense flooding to years of intense drought. See Queensland Government Department of Environment and Resource Management, Queensland Climate Change Centre of Excellence and Walker Institute, "Queensland Rainfall-past,

present and future," accessed November 25,2013. http://www.ehp.qld.gov.au/climatechange/centre/pdf/walker-report-summary-brochure.pdf.

5 Queensland Government, "South East Queensland," accessed November 25, 2013, http://www.qld.gov.au/about/about-queensland/towns/brisbane.

6 Delena Carbone and Jenna Hansen, "Floods: 10 of the deadliest in Australian History," *Australian Geographic*, January 29 2013, accessed August 15 2013, http://www.australiangeographic.com.au/journal/the-worst-floods-in-australian-history.htm.

7 Australian Government Bureau of Meteorology, "Queensland Flood Summary," accessed August 2, 2013, http://www.bom.gov.au/qld/flood/fld_history/floodsum_2010.shtml.

8 Queensland Government, "Budget Paper: Queensland's Natural Disasters 2013-2014," accessed August 2, 2013, http://www.budget.qld.gov.au/budget-papers/2013-14/queenslands-natural-disasters-2013-14.pdf.

9 Queensland Government, "Budget Paper, Queensland's Natural Disasters 2013-2014," 5, accessed August 2, 2013, http://www.budget.qld.gov.au/budget-papers/2013-14/queenslands-natural-disasters-2013-14.pdf.

10 Queensland Government, "Budget Paper, Queensland's Natural Disasters 2013-2014,"3, Queensland Government, accessed August 2, 2013, http://www.budget.qld.gov.au/budget-papers/2013-14/queenslands-natural-disasters-2013-14.pdf.

11 Australian Government, *Geoscience Australia*, "Where do Floods occur?" accessed August 2, 2013, http://www.ga.gov.au/hazards/flood/flood-basics/causes.html.

12 Australian Government, Geoscience Australia, "Where do Floods occur?" accessed August 2, 2013, http://www.ga.gov.au/hazards/flood/flood-basics/causes.html.

13 Tony Moore, "Council Salutes Mud Army," *Brisbane Times*, February 9, 2013, accessed November 25, 2013, http://www.brisbanetimes.com.au/queensland/council-salutes-mud-army-20110208-1altl.html.

14 Lauren Wilson, "State goes it alone in shunning insurance," *The Australian*, February 03, 2011, accessed August 2, 2013, http://www.theaustralian.com.au/in-depth/cyclone-yasi/state-goes-it-alone-in-shunning-insurance/story-fn7rj0ye-1225999067129.

15 Australian Government, Australian Taxation Office, "Flood levy information for individuals," accessed August 5, 2013, http://www.ato.gov.au/Individuals/Dealing-with-disasters/In-detail/Flood-levy/Flood-levy-information-for-individuals.

16 Commonwealth of Australia, National Disaster Insurance Review: inquiry into flood insurance and related matters, "Final Report: Executive Summary and Recommendations,"2011, 3, accessed August 11, 2013, http://www.ndir.gov.au/content/Content.aspx?doc=report.html.

17 Australian Government, The Treasury, "Government Response to Natural Disaster Insurance Review (NDIR) Recommendations," accessed August 11, 2011, http://www.treasury.gov.au/PublicationsAndMedia/Publications/2011/Government-Response-NDIR.html.

18 The United Nations Development Programme argues that human induced climate change is now wholly incontestable. See United Nations Development Programme, "A Climate Risk Management Approach to Disaster Reduction and Adaption to Climate Change," in *The Earthscan reader on adaptation to climate change*, ed. Lisa Schipper and Ian Burton, London; Sterling, VA: Earthscan, 2009, 230,35.

19 The Australian Government contests that the opportunity to avoid the effects of climate change has now passed, even if a significant reduction in greenhouse gasses is achieved. See Australian Government, "Adapting to Climate Change in Australia: An Australian Government Position Paper", 2010, 1-6, accessed August 2, 2013, www.climatechange.gov.au.

20 Australian Government, "Adapting to Climate Change in Australia: An Australian Government Position Paper", 2010, 1-6, accessed August 2, 2013, www.climatechange.gov.au.

21 In a little over two hundred years, the planet's population has increased from one billion to seven billion people, dramatically intensifying the risks associated with the occurrence of any disaster. Risk,according to Beck is not defined by catastrophe but is the anticipation of catastrophe and may then to some extent be predetermined and circumvented. See Ulrich Beck, *World at Risk*, Cambridge, UK ; Malden, MA: Polity Press, 2009, 186.

22 The Australian Government predicts that the continuation of current levels of global warming will result in increased temperatures, increases in the number of severe tropical cyclones along the Queensland coast, an increase in extreme rainfall events and a rise in sea levels, where a predicted rise of 1.1 meters would inundate between 35 and 60 thousand residential buildings in Queensland alone. See Australian Government, "Adapting to Climate Change in Australia: An Australian Government Position Paper", 2010, 27-30, 86-90, accessed August 2, 2013, www.climatechange.gov.au.

23 Marcus Moench, "Adapting to Climate Change and the Risks Associated with Other Natural Hazards: Methods for Moving from Concepts to Action," in *The Earthscan reader on adaptation to climate change*, ed. E. Lisa F. Schipper and Ian Burton, London; Sterling, VA: Earthscan, 2009, 256.

24 Marcus Moench, "Adapting to Climate Change and the Risks Associated with Other Natural Hazards: Methods for Moving from Concepts to Action," in *The Earthscan reader on adaptation to climate change*, ed. E. Lisa F. Schipper and Ian Burton, London: Sterling, VA: Earthscan, 2009, 187-94.

25 Tony Fry, "Metrofitting: A Statement of Position," in *Metrofitting: Adaptation, the City and Impacts of the Coming Climate*, Design Futures Working Paper No.1, in Fry et al, Brisbane: Queensland College of Art, Griffith University, 2009, 4-6.

26 In Bangladesh, a country prone to severe monsoonal flooding and two thirds of its land less than 5 meters above sea level, many thousands of lives and livelihoods are at risk from natural disaster each year. See "UN agencies helping Bangladesh, Myanmar prepare for Tropical Cyclone Mahasen," *UN News Centre*, May 15, 2011, accessed August 2, 2013, http://www.un.org/apps/news/story.asp?NewsID=44917&Cr=cyclone&Cr1= UN News-UN agencies helping Bangladesh, Myanmar prepare for Tropical Cyclone Mahasen.

27 Oxfam International "Bangladesh: Preparing for flood disaster," accessed August 3, 2013, http://www.oxfam.org/en/campaigns/climatechange/bangladesh-preparing-flood-disaster.

28 Local Government Association of Queensland, "Gympie Regional Council: Get Gympie Get Ready Resilience Program," accessed November 25, 2013, http://www.lgaq.asn.au/c/document_library/get_file?uuid=92a8f723-3d9b-4cff-aaed-294be4937bc7&groupId=10136.

29 Local Government Association of Queensland, "Community Development Engagement Initiative," accessed November 25, 2013, http://www.lgaq.asn.au/c/document_library/get_file?uuid=92a8f723-3d9b-4cff-aaed-294be4937bc7&groupId=10136.

30 Green Cross Australia, Harden Up Protecting Queensland, accessed November 25, 2013, http://hardenup.org.

31 Lockyer Valley Regional Council, "Strengthening Grantham Project Saves Community Millions," February 6, 2013, accessed November 25, 2013, http://www.lockyervalley.qld.gov.au/news-events/news/1575-strengthening-grantham-project-saves-community-millions.

32 Lockyer Valley Regional Council, "Australian-first Deal to Relocate Grantham Residents," May 5, 2011, accessed November 25, 2013,http://www.lockyervalley.qld.gov.au/news-events/news/1318-australian-first-deal-to-relocate-grantham-residents.

33 Kathy McLeish, "Community Project Puts Heart Back Into Grantham," *ABC News*, June 28, 2013, accessed November 25, 2013, "http://www.abc.net.au/news/2013-06-28/community-project-puts-heart-back-into-grantham/4789110.

RESILIENCE

THE URBAN LANDSCAPE AS A SOCIAL-ECOLOGICAL SYSTEM

by KRISHNA BHARATHI

Although twentieth century representations of the urban landscape have predominantly been divided between the 'built environment' and its surrounding 'naturalized landscape,' a wider range of imagery has gained traction in recent decades. These descriptions span multiple scales and conceive of the building stock: as a collective research object;[1] as protected heritage structures in relation to larger landscapes;[2] as systems of manmade artifacts which are slowly evolving and have long-term impacts while changing in use and form;[3] in addition to more essential depictions which recognize the urban landscape as a mediator between man and the elements.[4] Surveyed collectively, these characterizations resonate in varying degrees with facets of the concept of resilience; a perspective that has been employed in greater frequency across a broad cross-section of disciplines and to date has been most associated with the "ability of an element to return to a stable state after a disruption."[5] In regard to the urban landscape, resilience thinking asserts that the boundary conditions separating urban settlements from their wider environs is on a certain level artificial and would be better understood as parts of a multi-scalar dynamic that share a spatial and temporal interplay.[6]

Primarily developed to better understand the origins of both stability and instability in complex systems,[7] with the aim of developing capabilities to better anticipate, adapt and modify human actions in relation to change,[8] Martin-Breen and Anderies observe that:

> Increasingly one finds it [resilience] in political science, business administration, sociology, history, disaster planning, urban planning, and international development. The shared use of the term does not, however, imply unified concepts of resilience nor the theories in which it is embedded. Different uses generate different methods, sometimes different methodologies. Evidential or other empirical support can differ between domains of application, even when concepts are broadly shared.[9]

Untitled (Palast der Republik # 28), 2007 © Frank Thiel and VG Bild-Kunst, Bonn

This is a crucial point that underscores the often necessarily mixed application of resilience thinking to the urban landscape. Frequently, there is a tendency, especially within development and maintenance oriented tasks, for engineering and economic notions of resilience to be prioritized; approaches which contain embedded assumptions about behavior and intended outcomes such as return time, efficiency, and the ability to maintain functionality despite shocks with a focus on recovery, constancy, persistence, robustness. This differs from social-ecological resilience, which emphasizes cross-scale interactions, reorganization and development with a focus on adaptive capacity, transformability, learning and, innovation.[10]

Thus the critical difference between engineering and social-ecological notions of resilience rests in the mechanistic framing of behavior in the latter, which foregrounds a restoration to 'normal conditions' or 'bouncing back' after for example, physical infrastructure being subjected to stress. In contrast, social-ecological readings of resilience are opposed to being predictive[11] and emphasize the potential for multiple states of equilibrium,[12] which simultaneously opens up space for social critique and reflection. Thus, in this essay it is argued that reconsidering the urban fabric through the lens of social-ecological resilience can provide opportunities to both broaden and ground how designers' understand complexity within the interconnected narratives of design which ultimately engage social attitudes toward programmatic prioritization, land use, development and the disparity between regional consumption practices.

Social-Ecological Resilience

According to the Stockholm Resilience Center a social-ecological system or SES represents "linked systems of people and nature," and is a term that Fikret Berkes and Carl Folke developed in 1998 to attribute social and ecological dimensions equal weighting in their analyses.[13] In this context resilience relates to the scope of disturbance that a system can accommodate before it transitions to a different state that is directed by yet a different set of processes[14] or how the conditions which support a specific way of living can change over time to support an alternate set of conditions.[15] Most frequently the approach has been used in the management and governance of natural resources such as for example marine life, water harvesting, landscape preservation and food production. However, increasingly SES thinking is seen as being capable of contributing to the urban context by foregrounding dimensions of interactive complexity that have been largely absent from pre-resilience ecological theories, which emphasized depictions of the 'balance of nature.'

Therefore many of the terms used in the SES approach are derived from Brian Walker and C.S. Holling's ecological theory of resilience, which is organized around a single structural heuristic: the adaptive cycle and four behavioral heuristics of: panarchy or cross-scale interaction, resilience, adaptability and transform-ability. In brief, it is argued the adaptive cycle can be conceptualized as both the structural framework and the base building block of the system represented in the form of a figure eight, and the diagram consists of four, quarter phases: conservation, release, reorganization and growth. Additionally it is important to note that all of the phases and behaviors of the adaptive cycle do not necessarily manifest sequentially. Lastly, the interactions highlight the dynamic cross-scale potential of the panarchy heuristic whose multi-scalar relationships are not strictly linear or hierarchical through time or space.

For designers, social-ecological systems thinking has the potential to add another level of sophistication to how resource use and long range planning is integrated into the conceptual design of their projects. For example, in Moffat and Kohler's work on "Conceptualizing the built environment as a social-ecological system," the authors propose the incorporation of SES thinking in the analysis of a multi-parcel housing settlement through the use of "a balanced system perspective, which recognizes that "within a closed material realm, all flows between nature and built environments must be balanced over the long term."[16] Operationally this meant stretching the product related life cycle analysis (LCA) timeline typically associated with such efforts and instead, using mass flow accounting (MFA) to assess "aggregated physical flows" in and out of the development. This approach also included hidden flows to account for the total sum of materials not physically involved in the economic output under consideration, but implicated in processes linked to its material production, use, maintenance and disposal.[17]

Although providing the benefit of transparency and generating "an exceptional method for revealing system dynamics for the built environment at any scale, from parcel to urban region,"[18] the authors acknowledge that accounting tools such as MFA and LCA are segregated from key aspects of spatial design. Critically, their static conception of architectural/urban scale "affects the understanding of relationships between the built environment and the material world, on one side, and between the built environment and society, on the other."[19] That is, these methods reflect specific assumptions in their calculation methodologies and more problematically are not actively coupled to ongoing design processes in flux. Despite the recognition of the shortcomings existing in the available tools used, the primary contribution of this work indicates that when considered within a broader planning horizon, social-ecological resilience thinking can function as a viable theoretical foil to identify which factors are relevant for both large scale planning developments, as well as smaller interventions. In short, resilience thinking provides conceptual opportunities

for designers to contextualize their efforts by incorporating interdisciplinary, environmental concerns into the earlier, more strategic phases of their design work.

However, understandably these concepts appear to have a limited ability to describe the influence of technological phenomenon interacting within the sphere of the urban landscape, since as previously noted depending on the interpretation of the terms of resilience, adaptability and transformability, the conclusions may or may not constitute an environmentally balanced assessment of existing technological systems. For example Hommels observes that cities contain embedded obdurate processes which behave in a distinctly different fashion than natural settings lacking human intervention.[20] For example this behavior is evident in, but not limited to challenges which arise from: integrating older systems (e.g. sewer, transportation, power, etc.) with newer ones; developing pedestrian and public transportation access within cities dominated by sprawl and pervasive car infrastructure; or even the friction between strong building/landscape preservation lobbies

and political initiatives to renovate public infrastructure using newer technologies and construction techniques. Essentially, each of these examples illustrates that within the urban landscape, resilience is often understood to be "more about robustness to change and not about resilience for transformation."[21]

The Urban Landscape As A Social-Ecological System?

It is an obvious question to ask. Can the urban landscape legitimately be considered a social-ecological system (SES)? The short answer is yes, the longer answer no, and upon further reflection the answer cycles back to yes, with restrictions. The strength of the SES idea is that it places humanity within a system of interconnected activities, and the urban landscape can be understood as a physical manifestation of human activities. According to Folke et al. a SES is about the interdependency of systems of people and nature that foregrounds balanced integration.[22] However, as previously mentioned the behaviors of the working technical apparatus affiliated with urban settlements are often at odds with the metaphoric casting of the city as a social-ecological system. For example, in his critique of the deterministic narrative that argues that the pervasiveness presence of the automobile in American cities

was inevitable, urban historian McShane observes that automotive technologies developed out of changes in its urban culture and that subsequently, this irrevocably altered how cities were planned.[23] The work suggests that collective social choices, which support specific technologies over others, more accurately reflect the workings of socio-technical and socio-political processes, rather than social-ecological ones. Simply put, the current construction and intended focus of social-ecological theories are less capable of addressing issues of power, agency and choice - each integral dimensions of how societies are understood and structured.

Similar to the concept of sustainability, the unexamined trend of the rhetorical interchangeability of the term and the concept of resilience is a centrally problematic concern. That is, the concept's potential to clarify becomes blunted when the term is used ubiquitously. It is not to say that conceptualizing the urban landscape as a social-ecological system is not valuable. It is however, critical for designers to be aware that the application of social-ecological principles to the development of the urban landscape must necessarily extend beyond a simplistically opaque use of the term resilience. Additionally, designers should be aware that in its current iterations, resilience thinking is limited in its ability to address the range of socio-technical and socio-political processes that are intrinsic to the workings of the city, which often strongly direct development trajectories once certain critical decisions are made.[24] In other words, the decisions we make as designers, as consumers and ultimately as citizens have socio-technical and socio-political implications beyond the existing analytical scope of the resilience paradigm. For example, it has been observed that in Canada "greenhouse gas emissions and energy consumption per capita continue to increase," despite the fact that "best practices are borrowed from countries around the globe, green certifications are becoming the norm in architecture, public transportation systems are being built, and eco-communities develop."[25] This underscores how environmental agendas have translated primarily into the development of "buildings and systems that pollute, contaminate, and deplete less than their predecessors," and are simply becoming "more efficient at the wrong thing," which according to McDonough and Braungart is inherently more dangerous, since it erroneously suggests "environmental progress."[26] Here, the authors are also critiquing rote managerial approaches to how environmental heuristics are applied to design and SES thinking can be understood along the same lines, since social and environmental concerns undeniably link to political and technical ones within the context of the urban landscape.

Though the definition of social-ecological systems has been relaxed in recent literature to extend "beyond ecosystem services to include technological use of

natural resources such as minerals," it is widely understood in the literature that "the focus of socio-technical
transitions research is different from social-ecological
systems research in a number of respects" that include,
"objects, objectives, structure or function, and resilience
and transformation,"[27] and researchers Smith and Stirling surmise that, "understandably, the social-ecological
systems literature rarely considers the dynamics of
technological change in any detail." The authors continue, arguing the value of assessing both social-ecological
and socio-technical systems in tandem, since each is
"understood to display complex, dynamic, multi-scale,
and adaptive properties" and can "emphasize learning,
experimentation, and iteration."[28] Centrally, their aim is
for those using resilience to remain cognizant of "the
differences between the two areas of study, in terms
of problem framings and intellectual histories" in order
to "carefully and fruitfully" interpret the significance of
similarities.[29] In their analysis of social-ecological readings, the authors highlight the critical difference in the
structural and functional resilience of socio-technical

structures such as the built environment. In the quotation below the term 'regime' refers to a set of accepted
norms or rules:

> The particular socio-technical structures that are
> judged best in delivering requisite sustainability
> functions are often emphatically not the existing
> structures. It is thus intrinsic to socio-technical tran-
> sitions that functional sustainability is best achieved
> through structural transformation. Incumbent
> sociotechnical regimes are, by definition, structur-
> ally resilient. When regimes are no longer able to
> withstand shocks and stresses, they become desta-
> bilized... This process of decline and susceptibility to
> transformation renders them no longer regime-like.
> This intrinsic separability of structural and func-
> tional resilience remains to be fully appreciated in
> social-ecological research.[30]

Similarly, Voß incisively observes that "to ignore the
complexity and uncertainty that is involved in long-term

Untitled (Palast der Republik # 13), 2004 © Frank Thiel and VG Bild-Kunst, Bonn

structural change across the boundaries of society, technology and nature would mean to produce knowledge that is inadequate for the problem," and speculates "that simple models of reality and the forceful implementation of strategies that have been derived from them is one of the main roots of the problem of sustainable development."[31] So as designers, if we are to "redress the imbalance" in consumption and "embrace a wider view of the built environment"[32] using social-ecological resilience thinking, more work needs to be done in order to further develop how the structural and functional resilience of structures are understood within the urban landscape.

That is, the use of social-ecological resilience by the design professions additionally requires critical engagement on the part of designers to guide how structural and functional resilience can be both meaningfully operationalized and respon-sibility implemented.

People really are interdependent - saying nature is over there and people are here is a false perception resulting from our hubris in believing that we can control and use nature to our benefit for the foreseeable future. This in turn has allowed urbanization and a higher living standard, but at the cost of a loss of contact with nature, and is challenging the capacity of the life-supporting ecosystems to sustain our own development.[33]

Clearly there are no simple solutions or methodologies, but as the urban landscape reflects a turgid mix of interests, it is only fitting to concurrently frame social-ecological concerns in relation to their techno-political contexts. Insofar as the notion of social-ecological resilience advocates holistic thinking that encourages "critical reflection centered on disclosing the problem of the problem,"[34] it is a valuable conceptual tool to provoke and supplement design thinking in the studio.

	THE 5 HEURISTICS	MEANING	SOURCE
STRUCTURE	1. Adaptive Cycle	A concept which represents the internal dynamics and external influences of systems through four cyclical phases and depicted as a 'Figure 8.' Includes growth, conservation, release and reorganization. Multiple potentially stable states.	Gunderson and Holling 2002
		All phases of the adaptive cycle do not apply to all situations and alternative sequences have been identified which can involve: 1) no growth, 2) no conservation, 3) no structural reorganization, and 4) persistent phases.	Walker et al. 2006
BEHAVIOR	2. Panarchy	Encompasses multi-scalar processes from global to local, both accelerated and slow moving that can be perceived as gradual or episodic. Central to the concept is simultaneous cross-scale connections.	Holling et al. 2002
		The interactive dynamics of a nested set of adaptive cycles.	Folke et al. 2010
	3. Resilience	The capacity of a system to absorb disturbance and reorganize while undergoing change so as to still retain essentially the same function, structure and feedbacks, and therefore identity, that is, the capacity to change in order to maintain the same identity.	Folke et al. 2010
		Should be considered in terms of what govern the system's dynamics	Walker et al. 2004
		Multi-scale resilience : Fundamental for understanding the interplay between persistence and change, adaptability and transformability. Without the scale dimension, resilience and transformation may seem to be in stark contrast or even conflict.	Folke et al. 2010
		General resilience : The resilience of any and all parts of a system to all kinds of shocks, including novel ones.	Folke et al. 2010
		Specified resilience : The resilience "of what, to what"; resilience of some particular part of a system, related to a particular control variable, to one or more identified kinds of shocks.	Folke et al. 2010
		4 Aspects of resilience : Can be applied to the whole system and/or the sub-systems. 1) Latitude - Maximum amount a system can vary before losing its ability to recover. 2) Resistance - The ease or difficulty of changing a system. 3) Precariousness - How close the current state of the system is to a limit or threshold. 4) Panarchy - Nested systems with the capability to influence.	Walker et al. 2004
		Functional & response diversity : Functional diversity influences the performance of ecosystem components, or in the social domain actor groups. Response diversity or functional redundancy influences resilience.	Walker et al. 2006
	4. Adaptability	The capacity of the actors in a system to manage resilience.	Walker et al. 2004
		Primarily a function of the individuals and groups managing.	Walker et al. 2006
		Resilience and adaptability are closely related to the dynamics of a particular system.	Walker et al. 2004
	5. Transformability	Transformability refers to fundamentally altering the nature of a system.	Walker et al. 2004
		The capacity to transform the stability landscape itself in order to become a different kind of system, to create a fundamentally new system when ecological, economic, or social structures make the existing system untenable.	Folke et al. 2010 Walker et al. 2004, 2006
		Involves the three key factors of building knowledge, Networking & Leadership	Olsson et. al 2006
		Active transformation : The deliberate initiation of a phased introduction of one or more new state variables (i.e. such as a new way of making a living) at lower scales, while maintaining the resilience of the system at higher scales as transformational change proceeds.	Folke et al. 2010
		Forced transformation : An imposed transformation of a SES system that is not introduced deliberately by the actors.	Folke et al. 2010

ENDNOTES

1 N. Kohler and U. Hassler, "The building stock as a research object," *Building Research & Information* 30, 4 (2002): 226-236.

2 J. Pendlebury, *Conservation in the Age of Consensus* (Abingdon: Routledge, 2009).

3 R. Lowe, '"Preparing the built environment for climate change," *Building Research & Information* 31, 4-5 (2003) 195-199.

4 S. Rintala, "Edge On Paracentric Architecture," *Topos* 70 (2010): 48-55.

5 R. Bhamra, S. Dani and K. Burnard, "Resilience: the concept, a literature review and future directions," *International Journal of Production Research* 49, 19 (2011): 5376.

6 Folke, C., S. Carpenter, B. Walker, M. Scheffer, T. Chapin, and J. Rockstrom. "Resilience thinking: integrating resilience, adaptability and transformability." *Ecology and Society* 15, 4 (2010). http://www.ecologyandsociety.org/vol15/iss4/art20/.

7 Peeples, M, C. Barton, and S. Schmich. "Resilience lost: intersecting land use and landscape dynamics in the prehistoric southwestern United States." *Ecology and Society* 11, 22 (2006). http://www.ecologyandsociety.org/vol11/iss2/art22/

8 Buizer, M., B. Arts, and K. Kok. "Governance, scale, and the environment: the importance of recognizing knowledge claims in transdisciplinary arenas." *Ecology and Society* 16, 21 (2011). http://www.ecologyandsociety.org/vol16/iss1/art21/.

9 Martin-Breen, P., and J.M. Anderies. "Resilience: A Literature Review." Rockefeller Foundation (2011) http://www.rockefellerfoundation.org/news/publications/resilience-literature-review, 5.

10 C. Folke, "Resilience: the emergence of a perspective for social-ecological systems analysis," *Global Environmental Change* 16 (2006): 259.

11 Peeples, M. C. Barton, and S. Schmich. "Resilience lost: intersecting land use and landscape dynamics in the prehistoric southwestern United States."

12 Folke, C., and L. Gunderson. "Facing global change through social-ecological research." *Ecology and Society* 11, 2 (2006). http://www.ecologyandsociety.org/vol11/iss2/art43/.

13 http://www.stockholmresilience.org/21/research/what-is-resilience/resilience-dictionary.html

14 Carpenter et al. (2001)

15 Hughes, T.P., Carpenter, S., Rockström, S., Scheffer, M., Walker, B. 2013. "Multiscale regime shifts and planetary boundaries." *Trends in Ecology & Evolution* 28, 7 (2013).

16 S. Moffatt, and N. Kohler, "Conceptualizing the built environment as a social ecological system," *Building Research & Information* 36, 3 (2008): 254ff.

17 Ibid.

18 Ibid., 256.

19 Ibid., 257.

20 A. Hommels, "Studying obduracy in the city: Toward a productive fusion between technology studies and urban studies," *Science, Technology & Human Values* 30 (2005): 323-351.

21 C. Folke et. al. "Resilience thinking: integrating resilience, adaptability and transformability." *Ecology and Society* 15, 4 (2010). http://www.ecologyandsociety.org/vol15/iss4/art20/, 6.

22 Ibid., 2.

23 C. McShane. *Down the asphalt path: The automobile and the American city.* (New York, Columbia University Press: 1994).

24 A. Hommels, "Studying obduracy in the city: Toward a productive fusion between technology studies and urban studies," *Science Technology and Human Values* 30 (2005): 323-351.

25 C. Déprés, G. Vachon and A. Fortin. 2011. "Implementing Transdisciplinarity: Architecture and Urban Planning at Work," in *Transdisciplinary knowledge production in architecture and urbanism, Towards hybrid modes of inquiry*, eds. Isabelle Doucet and Nel Janssens, (Vienna: Springer, 2011), 33f.

26 W. McDonough, and M. Braungart, "Eco-Effectiveness: A New Design Strategy," in *Sustainable Architecture: White Papers*, eds. D. Brown, M. Fox, M.R. Pelletier. (NY: Earth Pledge Foundation, 2005). 1f.

27 Smith, A., and A. Stirling. "The politics of social-ecological resilience and sustainable socio-technical transitions." *Ecology and Society* 15, 1 (2010). http://www.ecologyandsociety.org/vol15/iss1/art11/, 3.

28 Ibid., 1.

29 Ibid., 6.

30 Ibid., 4.

31 J. Voß, "Shaping socio-ecological transformation: The case for innovating governance" (paper presented at the Open Science Meeting of the International Human Dimensions Programme of Global Environmental Change Research, Montreal, Canada October 18, 2003) 6.

32 R. Lorch, "A research strategy for the built environment?" *ARQ* 7, no. 2 (2003): 121.

33 C. Folke, "How resilient are ecosystmes to global environmental change," *Sustainability Science* 5 (2010): 153.

34 T. Fry, "Getting over architecture: Thinking, surmounting and redirecting," in *Transdisciplinary knowledge production in architecture and urbanism: Towards hybrid modes of inquiry*, eds. Isabelle Doucet and Nel Janssens (New York: Springer, 2011), 21.

Map of Multi-Family Housing Concentrations in Houston

MULTI-FAMILY HOUSING IN AN ERA OF CHANGE

THE NEW PROJECTS

by SUSAN ROGERS

... the poor would make do, somehow, as they always did.
Marshall Berman *All That is Solid Melts Into Air: The Experience of Modernity, 1982*

While the old public housing "projects" have been demolished in Chicago to make way for saccharine sweet new urbanist style mixed-income neighborhoods—in cities like Houston (and suburbs throughout the U.S.) disinvestment, changing desires, and shifting socio-economic and spatial conditions are combining to create the "new projects" on the periphery. The new projects look nothing like the old: most were built quickly and cheaply in the 1970s and 1980s, most often for young professionals, isolated and disconnected from the surrounding city and with little green space or amenities. In Houston these projects are increasingly home to more families than singles and a growing number of people who live below the poverty line. Simultaneously, these units are quickly deteriorating, having reached the end of a typical investment cycle and in the absence of a national housing policy, where vouchers comprise the

largest portion of low-income housing subsidies, represent a new de-facto public housing.

315,357—is the number of multi-family apartments in Houston housed in buildings comprised of ten or more units. This housing is home to just under one million people. 150,000 of these units were constructed between 1960 and 1980, a period of rapid growth. Over the last four decades these units have churned quickly through three stages of Holling and Gunderson's adaptive cycle—exploitation, conservation, and release. Some, but by no means all, are now moving through a reorganization period, the fourth stage, and with this evidence of adaptive capacity and resiliency are emerging.[1] Pools are filled-in to eliminate risks for children; units are gutted and transformed into community centers, places of worship, small businesses, and after-school programs. Courtyards are fenced to provide small

though functional space for children's games. Furniture is moved outside transforming the outdoors into an extension of the home.

As a means to explore the adaptive capacity of multi-family housing, two Houston complexes serve as case studies. What binds these complexes together is the age of the units, the disconnection of the complexes from the surrounding neighborhood, and the shifting demographics. What sets the complexes apart are different levels of social and community organization, economic investment, ecology—particularly in relationship to density and mixed-uses—and adaptive capacity.

St. Cloud is a quiet oasis in the center of one of Houston's densest, poorest, and most diverse neighborhoods—Gulfton. But this is not the inner city, it is the periphery—and St. Cloud is not a tenement, it is a simple garden apartment complex—one of nearly 50 similar complexes in a three-square mile area that combined total 15,000 units. Gulfton, once a prime destination for young professional singles moving to the city in the 1970s, began transforming in the late 1980s when Houston's economy collapsed with the price of oil. As single professionals moved on to greener pastures, new immigrants began arriving in the city and filling the vacated units. Today more than 60% of Gulfton residents were born outside the U.S., and poverty sits at a staggering 39%. But St. Cloud, along with other complexes in the neighborhood, stands in defiance of expectations and has emerged as a model for adaptive strategies.

Sited on a superblock over 600' in length, St. Cloud is an island, gated and set apart from the surrounding neighborhood. The repeating pattern of courtyards and parking areas are framed by two-story buildings that open to the front and back. At one time there were four pools; all of them have been filled in. Two factors have shaped change and adaptation in the complex. First, the property owners have been active in carrying out improvements—including upgrading air conditioners to energy efficient units and more creative ideas such as installing tall fences in one of the courtyards so youth can play soccer and other sports without breaking adjacent windows. Two units have also been transformed into community spaces, one an after-school program and the other an adult education center. Second, the residents, nearly all immigrants from Bhutan and Nepal, share common cultures and languages and through these bonds have created a community. Men gather in the courtyard to play the traditional board game carrom, children play freely in the courtyards, chairs are moved outside to supervise, and pickling jars and container gardens dot balconies and carports. Finally, the dense neighborhood outside the boundaries of the property has all of the basic necessities.

Built in 1976, the complex now known as Thai Xuan Village was originally the Cavalier Apartments. The development's complex history, cycling through decline and renewal, weaves a powerful story of resilience. Located on the south side of Houston, Thai Xuan Village is one of twenty separate apartment complexes lining a one-mile corridor of Broadway near Hobby Airport. In the 1980s the area had begun to lose its luster, and flight attendants and other young professionals moved on. In 1993 a Vietnamese Catholic priest, Father John Chinh Tran bought the complex, renamed it Thai Xuan Village, and invited new refugees from South Vietnam to live there. A few years later the complex was sold to residents as condominiums, many today valued between $5,000 and $10,000.

Over the next fifteen years the complex deteriorated, balconies sagged, railings collapsed, and broken windows hinted at escalating decline. In 2007 elected officials, responding to pressure from neighboring community leaders, began threatening the owners with demolition. The residents fought back, organized a tenant organization, and in 2009 secured $250,000 in affordable housing funds to upgrade the complex. The sagging balconies are once again plumb, roofs have been repaired, and the exterior has been painted and cleaned. Today, Thai Xuan Village is a story of organized change and resiliency – a small outdoor chapel sits in the courtyard adja cent to a filled in pool, tenants grow vegetables and fruits in their small yards or on the balconies, and children play basketball on the slab of a demolished building. As Josh Harkinson writes in the *Houston Press*:

Any sidewalk between any two buildings leads into a valley of micro farms crammed with herbs and vegetables that would confound most American botanists. Entire front yards are given over to choy greens. Mature papaya trees dangle green fruit overhead, and vines sagging with wrinkled or spiky melons climb trellises up second-story balconies. Perfumed night jasmine stretches for light alongside trees heavy with satsumas, limes, and calamondins. Where the soil ends, Vietnamese mints and peppers sprout out of anything that will contain roots . . . [2]

There are two options for the future of the new projects: demolish or adapt. The powerful are pushing for demolition, which would create a 21st century re-development opportunity at a scale not witnessed since urban renewal. Yet, quietly throughout Houston, innovative models for adaptation are emerging – complexes and apartments are retrofitted for charter schools, places of worship, community centers, small businesses, and youth programs. Gardens, sports fields, and gathering places have transformed formerly ornamental green spaces into useful areas. Social organization is strengthening in complexes where it is nurtured and supported by the physical infrastructure. And new funding programs for the renovation of aging

multi-family complexes are emerging on the national front. Yet, more needs to be done. Documenting success, either organic or planned, is part of the solution; understanding failure is the second part. Defining a methodology to adapt multi-family complexes has the potential to preserve hundreds of thousands of affordable housing units and push against the possibility of future failure and demolition.

ENDNOTES

1 Gunderson, Lance H. and C.S. Holling, "Resilience and the Adaptive Cycle," in Lance H. Gunderson and C.S. Holling, eds., *Panarchy, Understanding Transformations in Human and Natural Systems*. (Washington D.C.: Island Press, 2002). Page 34.

2 Harkinson, Josh, "Tale of Two Cities," (*Houston Press*, December 15, 2005). Available at http://www.houstonpress.com/2005-12-15/news/tale-of-two-cities/.

Thai Xuan Village
Broadway

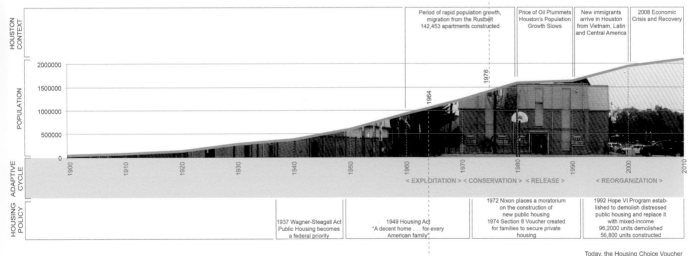

| HOUSTON CONTEXT | | | | | | | | Period of rapid population growth, migration from the Rustbelt 142,453 apartments constructed | | Price of Oil Plummets Houston's Population Growth Slows | New immigrants arrive in Houston from Vietnam, Latin and Central America | 2008 Economic Crisis and Recovery |

POPULATION

2000000
1500000
1000000
500000
0

1976
1964

1900 1910 1920 1930 1940 1950 1960 1970 1980 1990 2000 2010

ADAPTIVE CYCLE

< EXPLOITATION > < CONSERVATION > < RELEASE > < REORGANIZATION >

HOUSING POLICY

1937 Wagner-Steagall Act Public Housing becomes a federal priority

1949 Housing Act "A decent home . . . for every American family"

1972 Nixon places a moratorium on the construction of new public housing
1974 Section 8 Voucher created for families to secure private housing

1992 Hope VI Program established to demolish distressed public housing and replace it with mixed-income
96,2000 units demolished
56,800 units constructed

Today, the Housing Choice Voucher program provides assistance to 2.1 million low-income families. In Houston the waiting list for a voucher was re-opened for the first time in six years in August 2012. 83,743 families applied to be placed on a waiting list to secure one of 20,000 vouchers.

St. Cloud
Gulfton

EXILED

SPATIAL IDENTITIES OF THE TIBETAN DIASPORA

by GREGORY MARINIC

For displaced communities, commercial and cultural activities introduce shared narratives within an unfamiliar built environment. Typically relying upon existing buildings, these interventions are sown primarily as spatial, interior and adaptive gestures. However, the most significant and lasting appropriations are often authored by those who do not have the option of return. In *The Production of Space*, Henri Lefebvre engaged daily life as a theoretical critique of architecture. By observing that space is a social construct based on values, practices, perceptions and production, he advocated for a critical shift in spatial discourse. Identifying processes of incrementalism and multiplicity of authorship, Lefebvre asserts that cities and buildings are ultimately subjected to human needs, daily routines and conventional social practices. As a dialectical or humanist Marxist who was highly critical of the abstract and a-historical structuralism that dominated his era, Lefebvre argued that everyday manipulations of space are fundamental to the growth of cities and thus to capitalism itself. In this sense, such *interventions* act as agents of resilience within the contemporary city. Viewed through this Lefebvrian lens, the participatory nature of adapted buildings interrogates cycles of consumption and fashion that have increasingly reduced architecture to self-absorbed authorship.[1]

This essay explores resilience and heterotopian narratives—or spaces of a shared ethnic or cultural experience—based on compromise, the search for familiarity amid exile and the remaking of buildings in the New York neighborhood of Jackson Heights, Queens. Modest community needs shape architectures of the everyday, framing spatial identities based on an accessible trove of existing buildings, mobile structures and light architectures. Here, adaptive re-use has supported the re-emergence of a community far from its place of origin. Bridging past and present, Tibetan exiles have forged new identities within the finely grained streets of Jackson Heights. Surveying various repurposed fixed and mobile architectures—specifically those used for commercial, cultural and spiritual activities of the Tibetan diaspora—this essay reveals forces of transnationalism, contextual hybridization and territorialization. It examines the role of "exiled" architectures in the incremental re-making of Jackson Heights into a resilient and temporal Tibetan heterotopia in North America.

Spatial Production & Otherness

The reality of everyday life resists the unilateral commodification of the built environment, yet continues to share similar qualities of impermanence, identity and commercialization. Engaging the quotidian through theoretical observation, Lefebvre states that space is a social product based on values, practices, perceptions and production. His argument suggests a critical shift in spatial perspective by identifying multi-faceted processes of production that embrace multiplicity of authorship.[2] This approach implies distrust of the heroic and fashionable, as well as suspicion of architecture that serves commodification.[3] Thus, by reframing architecture through remarkably understated practices and the impact of people reshaping buildings, Lefebvre celebrates the commonplace, ordinary and unschooled manipulations that buildings and cities receive apart from the pedigreed top-down hands of architects, designers and planners.[4] Similarly, Colin Ward, a renowned social theorist, applauded built environments that percolate up rather than trickle down since they

Evidence of the Tibetan community in Queens

result in higher self-sufficiency, better organization and increased resilience.

Both Lefebvre and Ward fixed their gazes upon the lives of buildings well beyond the moment of their completion. Unlike the formalized rituals of Architecture and Urban Planning, everyday manipulations are anonymous, layered, imprecise and unstructured, and therefore difficult to quantify due to their irregularity and bottom-up emergence. Disorganized and fragmented, they are imperfect, organic and authentic. These transformations reflect past usage patterns while revealing the subtleties of more recent shifts. Much like the upheaval of displaced persons, adapted buildings reveal imperfect circumstances and disordered spatiality—and thus each offers the other a potential for new life.

Resilience and Heterotopias

Modest and informal practices, leveraged through existing buildings, are often engaged by immigrant communities as they carve out space within unfamiliar territories. Emphatically un-monumental, anti-heroic and autonomous, these transformations reflect limited means, as well as the impact of time and collective memory.[5] Considering immigration and the urban neighborhood, *everyday* architecture and the re-use of buildings may be linked to heterotopia. However, unlike utopias that architecturally occupy "no place", heterotopias exist as idealized places of otherness connecting common people with new experiences and unfamiliar physical places. Heterotopias satisfy the basic human desire to mark and redefine space. They are inherently contingent upon compromise. They are adaptive and contribute to the process of building resilience.

Foucault employed the term *heterotopia* to describe such places and spaces that blend multi-faceted layers of meaning, as well as connectivity to other places. These worlds of otherness—which are neither here nor there— engage physical, mental and phenomenological characteristics associated with memory.[6] Appropriating aspects of idealism gleaned from lives lost and past realities, heterotopias represent the physical manifestation and approximation of idealism among a shared people. For the Tibetan community living outside of the historical borders of Tibet, these heterotopias have become more than mere outposts. Rather, these discontinuous territories have become a "New Tibet" which supplants the old, supports the new and waits for a national resurgence of the homeland.

From Marginalization to Stabilization and Resilience

Researchers, scholars and practitioners in various disciplines have struggled with the notion of *resilience* in their respective fields for decades.[7] The idea of fostering resilience in the infrastructure of our cities is a strategic theme and operational goal for many communities around the world.[8] As architects, designers and planners struggle to develop prescriptive models that guide resilient practices—the ecological, economic and social dimensions of resilience have become increasingly more evident within established urban forms. More recently, the focus on resilience marks a shift away from anticipation of risk and mitigation and toward a more integrated model that promotes protective and preventative strategies.[9] Conventional or low-tech approaches to *resistance* may be tethered to the more responsive and regenerative aspects of *resilience*.[10] It is the adaptive nature of existing buildings that systematizes a bottom-up framework of social support for exiles.

For marginalized populations in developing countries displaced by warfare, ecological collapse, natural disasters or political conflict, survival is based upon the community's ability to reorganize and remake itself socially and spatially. In developed countries such as the United States, complex distribution systems are now the primary means of supplying populations with food, water, housing and transportation. Communities build their everyday activities around various systems over which they have very little control. Power grids, computer systems and communication networks are, generally speaking, unprepared to cope with major disruptions to the flow of vital services, resources and infrastructures. Conventional efficiencies inherent within these complex systems reduce resilience through deficits in redundancy and diversity. However, in terms of the urban built environment and its existing building stock, resilience takes on a social dimension based upon re-use and re-investment, as well as the associated redundancies that mitigate the potential for collapse.

Adaptation in the Outer Boroughs

The modest residential neighborhoods in the outer boroughs of New York have been conceived over time by continuous worldwide flows of immigrants. These spaces and places have been embedded with the institutional memory of countless former lives. As such, New York City is an exceptionally well-tuned vehicle for embracing, supporting and assimilating successive and diverse communities. Across the five boroughs, various neighborhoods have rebounded after continual highs and lows—underscoring their enduring appeal as gateways, grounding places and homes. The neighborhood scale of the built environment is of particular importance to the social, economic and communal parameters of resilience. Offering new immigrants an ability to regroup and recover, these modest residential neighborhoods have been critically important to the most vulnerable—the exiled.

Exiled communities that do not have an option to return to their homelands must negotiate various polarities--chaos and order, ambivalence and adaptation, resistance and resilience--while continually learning and transforming within a new context. The built environments that exiled communities encounter in their new countries are not created equal and must be assessed as they pertain to a community's unique circumstances. The core attributes of resilient systems—resource diversity, resource performance, institutional memory, learning and connectivity—must be considered in relation to ecological, economic, infrastructural, social and political subsystems.[11] One of the most vital and central aspects of resilience in relation to displaced persons is the ability for neighborhoods to adequately support residential, commercial, social, spiritual and cultural needs.[12] In New York, the search for appropriate space is compounded by issues of affordability, crowding and age of buildings, as well as access to transportation and other like-minded communities.

Tibetan Vernaculars in Queens

Commercial buildings in the outer boroughs of New York range from the architecturally sophisticated to considerably more modest vernaculars. By the 1970s, new immigrants encountered a building stock which was not new: buildings had been adapted or reconstructed, and, in some cases, they had been abandoned or destroyed. As evidenced through diverse attitudes regarding building culture and building usage, the built environment of New York City is inherently hybridized and reflects immigrant settlement patterns which have imparted a continual shifting and blurring of cultural, social and architectural identities on the existing building stock.

As an indicator of assimilation within an American context, commercial districts reflect the status of an immigrant culture in New York. For Tibetans in Jackson Heights living among other groups from countries in Latin America and South Asia, existing building interventions are understated and ephemeral. Focused within one of the most international districts in Queens, the Tibetan community of Jackson Heights represents one of the largest settlements outside of Tibet. Here, the *storefront* typology provides a political, cultural and social mechanism for an economically diverse community. Clothing stores, trinket stalls, temples, restaurants and momo carts transform the streets of the neighborhood into a market town on the Trans-Himalayan plateau.

The everyday storefront falls into the category of non-pedigreed architecture, defined by its vernacular, spontaneous and anonymous development. Typically encountered as first floor retail spaces facing onto the street, storefronts are characterized by their neutrality, porousness and direct access. As a vernacular typology, the storefront falls into a quotidian architecture that develops informally and incrementally. It is an inherently *plug-in* system that offers quick-start territorialization, as well as the opportunity to blend seamlessly into pre-existing urban and social structures. Like other American storefront interventions, Tibetan commercial

and cultural endeavors react to quintessentially urban conditions—the existing commercial districts, street corners and building types of Jackson Heights.

As a temporal typology, the storefront vernacular of Jackson Heights remains largely undocumented; however, it simultaneously reveals past lives and creates new identities for the Tibetan diaspora. Commercial storefronts of the growing community serve specific needs for retail, sacred spaces, cultural organizations and restaurants. Existing building interventions, mobile architectures and exterior spatial manipulations evoke the graphic, polychromatic, aromatic and atmospheric memories of Lhasa. Blending into their adjacencies, these Tibetan interventions accept and adapt to the idiosyncrasies of the context of central Queens and create an ersatz-Tibetan street culture.

From Stewardship to Accretion and Assimilation

The assimilation of immigrants into new environments results in subtle and significant changes to normative spatial and architectural conditions. Existing buildings may be employed by new users as a platform upon which values and memories may be recast. This socio-architectural phenomenon is facilitated through the historical layers of time, the introduction of new interventions and the continuous overlapping of architectural strata. As such, the physical parameters of architecture as an *object* with a multi-faceted ontological structure may be correlated with the phenomenon of memory. Existing buildings act as performance spaces that reconstruct an emergent consciousness of the past. The newly acquired built environment thus reframes collective memories so that the community may address new conditions to gain traction and build resilience.

The organic modus operandi of architecture allows it to outlast individual phases. Supporting this notion, Cesare Brandi's theory of restoration states that architecture operates as a layered manifold and a timeless object.[13] Filtered from this perspective, the nomadic content of the built environment of Jackson Heights may be autonomously determined by subjects as a way to relive memories, to recast processes and to remake past events—oftentimes idealized—through regenerative interventions. In this sense, the adapted architectures of Little Tibet acts as a bridge between memory and culture through the building-up of old layers within an entirely new context.

Conclusion: Dislocation and Collective Memories in Little Tibet

French philosopher and sociologist Maurice Halbwachs (1877-1945) developed the concept of collective memory in his book "*La mémoire collective*" and examined how individuals and groups employ mental images of the present to reconstruct an edited vision of the past. Halbwachs asserted that human memory functions within a

collective context that is always selective.[14] For Halbwachs, individual memories are lived through shared experiences within a collective domain and are thus subjugated to the impact of outside influences. These conditions include traumatic physical dislocation and the re-establishment of memory within a new context.

As globalism shifts the conventional notion of "territory", the contemporary spatiality of many cultures has migrated toward the potential for ersatz-utopias, or heterotopias, far from home yet digitally tethered back to the homeland. The everyday adapted buildings of Jackson Heights offer an opportunity to witness exceptionally modest and informal approaches to remaking buildings. In the case of the Tibetan community, quotidian desires shape quintessentially ordinary and participatory architectures that blend collective, yet faded, memories of the past with a newly encountered built environment. Viewed from the perspective of displacement—time and temporality have profound implications in the on-going resilience of the Tibetan overseas diaspora. Searching for familiarity within a new land, the Tibetan cultural imprint on the contemporary built environment of Jackson Heights is undeniable and growing. It reveals nuances, hybridizations, aspirations and cross-pollinations that serve a bifurcated tradition that was dramatically exiled from the East and has incrementally matured in the West. These everyday building adaptations reflect the participatory and informal emergence of Tibetan cultural and political endurance, as well as the contradictory memories of a contentious past and uncertain future.

The twenty-first century Tibetan "architectures" of Jackson Heights are shaped not by architects, but by laypersons using modest means and the bottom-up potentialities offered by collaboration with various makers and stakeholders. They are spatial and temporal, they are ephemeral and mobile, and they are contingent upon affordability, practicality and compromise. In their rawest form, they sabotage conventional wisdoms and shift our expectations for what is possible here, in regulated North America. Furthermore, *exile* serves as the primary shaper of identity in the Tibetan community, underscoring resilience in terms of its cultural significance, as well as its agency in relation to building stewardship. Dependent upon an existing building stock, Tibetans have fostered economic advancement and assimilation, while simultaneously carving out greater autonomy. This autonomy—offered through the adaptive re-use of ordinary buildings--has resulted in a more pronounced and visible presence for the Tibetan diaspora in Queens. While the historic heart of the community remains in Jackson Heights, its influence has migrated far beyond the neighborhood to become a force in the regeneration of storefront spaces as a discontinuous residential, commercial and spiritual territory—a *New Tibet*— serving Tibetans, as well as other communities across the borough. The diaspora has contributed to the stewardship of existing buildings in Queens, as well as the broader socio-economic wellness of a multicultural community.

Experienced through one's own body moving through space and time, the participatory act of social engage-

Storefront vernacular, Jackson Heights

ment, particularly at times of political upheaval, cannot be underestimated. For exiled communities such as Little Tibet, the work of Maurice Halbwachs may be engaged to understand the new realities of Jackson Heights. Halbwachs asserts that dramatic dislocations engender displaced persons with a more intense awareness of its past and present, since the bonds attaching them to physical spaces gain greater clarity through their destruction.[15] Tibetan diasporic communities share the most profound and lasting mental memories of past physical landscapes. Violent political events transformed the relationship of this dislocated group to new places, resulting in heightened awareness and territoriality.[16] Giving rise to plurality in relation to both time and place, collective memories are most frequently remembered through physical manifestation—through the material rather than the temporal aspects of the

built environment. Halbwachs states that displaced persons pay disproportionate attention to the material aspects of their lost built environments.[17] He postulates that the great majority of people in this group tend to be more sensitive to the destruction of their physical environments, rather than to the larger political or religious conflicts that caused dislocation. In the case of Little Tibet and the larger national tragedy of Tibetans, a primarily adaptive and temporal phenomenon has grown unevenly throughout Jackson Heights. Modestly incremental accretions reveal subtleties of lost experiences, lost memories and lost spatialities. These nuanced yet radical shifts in sensibility have contributed to the building and rebuilding of the neighborhood—the architectural *palimpsest*—as a reappropriated and hetertopian ersatz Tibet.

ENDNOTES:

1 Deleuze, Gilles. 2002. "How Do We Recognise Structuralism?" In *Desert Islands and Other Texts 1953-1974.* Trans. David Lapoujade. Ed. Michael Taormina. Semiotext(e) Foreign Agents ser. Los Angeles and New York: Semiotext(e), 2004. 170–192

2 Lefebvre, Henri. *The Production of Space*, Donald Nicholson-Smith trans., Oxford: Basil Blackwell. Originally published in French.

3 John Sturrock (1979), *Structuralism and Since: from Lévi Strauss to Derrida.*

4 Lefebvre, Henri, *The Critique of Everyday Life, Volume 1*, John Moore trans., London: Verso. Originally published in 1945, reprinted in 1991.

5 Lefebvre, Henri with Catherine Regulier-Lefebvre *Eléments de rythmanalyse: Introduction à la connaissance des rythmes,* preface by René Lorau, Paris: Ed. Syllepse, Collection "Explorations et découvertes". English translation: *Rhythmanalysis: Space, time and everyday life,* Stuart Elden, Gerald Moore trans. Continuum, New York, 2004

6 Michel Foucault. *Of Other Spaces* (1967), Heterotopias. This text, entitled "Des Espace Autres," was published by the French journal *Architecture/Mouvement/ Continuité* in October, 1984. The text was the basis for a lecture given by Michel Foucault in March 1967. Although not reviewed for publication by the author and thus not part of the official corpus of his work, the manuscript was released into the public domain for an exhibition in Berlin shortly before Michel Foucault's death. It was translated from the French by Jay Miskowiec.

7 Maurice Halbwachs and Coser, Lewis A., *On Collective Memory,* 244 p. vols. (Chicago: University of Chicago Press, 1992). p. 75.

8 Maurice Halbwachs, *On Collective Memory,* 1st edition, Chicago: University of Chicago Press, 1992. English translation by Lewis A. Coser

9 Ibid. 122-135

10 Ibid. 142-154

11 Researchers in various disciplines have observed that allowing for diversification of resources is a vital aspect of developing resilience. When a system becomes more diverse, its complex interaction networks spread unevenly and its individual assets do not have the same effect on the diverse components. See, e.g., W. Brian Arthur, "On the Evolution of Complexity," in *Complexity: Metaphors, Models and Reality 19,* ed. G. Cowan, D. Pines, D. Meltzer (Santa Fe Institute Studies in the Sciences of Complexity Proceedings, 1995), 60-80. A successful strategy that increase the viability of individuals or groups in such a system will almost never be common, but shared redundancies within the infrastructure contribute to resilient practices serving all groups.

12 Resilience thinking was first developed in C.S. Holling, "Resilience and Stability of Ecological Systems," *Annual Review of Ecological Systems 4* (1973). See the Resilience Alliance website for further details: www.resalliance.org See L. Gunderson, C. Allen, and C.S. Holling (editors), Foundations of Ecological Resilience (Washington D.C.: Island Press, 2010).

13 S. Flynn, *The Edge of Disaster: Rebuilding a Resilient Nation* (New York: Random House, 2007).

14 B. Walker, C. S. Holling, S. R. Carpenter, and A. Kinzig, "Resilience, adaptability and transformability in social–ecological systems," *Ecology and Society 9* (2004).

15 Ibid.

16 Ibid.

17 "Objects that endure in time differ from events in that they are capable of lasting beyond the individual instants in which events, in a way, are locked, and they therefore endure longer than events. This is also true, however, of processes; hence, this does seem to be something [that is peculiarly] characteristic of the objects presently under consideration. Yet it is just in the way in which an enduring object outlasts individual instants that is shown its profound dissimilarity to processes. A process does this, namely, in this way: that the phase now actual passes into an entirely new, although not disjunct, phase, and extends into it continuously. But an enduring object remains identically the same through the constantly new instants in which it exists." Cfr. Cesare Brandi, *Teoria Del Restauro* (Torino: Einaudi, 1963), Cesare Brandi et al., *Theory of Restoration*, 186 p. vols. (Roma: Istituto centrale per il restauro, 2005).

New steps, Salemi

TAKING ON THE SHAPE OF THINGS

ROBERTO COLLOVÀ: THE SPIRIT OF RESILIENCE

EXCERPTS FROM AN INTERVIEW WITH INT/AR EDITOR
LILIANE WONG

The text of the full interview is available in its entirely as a PDF
http://intar-journal.risd.edu

For centuries, Sicily was the crossroad of western civilization. With a rich heritage that includes the Phoenicians, Greeks, Romans, Arabs, Normans, French, Germans, the history of Sicily and its many different inhabitants is a quintessential example of social resilience. As an island, it has demonstrated a remarkable ability for continuity, recovery and change. The work of architect Roberto Collovà in Sicily comprises architecture, urban design, landscape design, furniture design and photography. His projects, writing and photographs capture the resilient spirit of Sicily; from the bustle of Palermo to Gela, an historic town at the southern coast, transformed by industry and violence, and the western towns of Salemi and Gibellina, destroyed by earthquake and rebuilt. In its spare and poetic simplicity his work speaks of an endurance that is at the heart of Sicily and its peoples. I had the great fortune to meet and speak with him at his studio in Palermo.

Int|AR: What characterizes Sicily and its peoples that enables them to adjust, survive and thrive under different circumstances?

RC: Sicily is rich in artistic and literary patrimony, but each is relative to a colonization, and therefore, the beauty of art and architecture corresponds to different forms of domination. Often, justly intoxicated by beauty, we forget that the most impressive manifestations of human work in history correspond to periods where power resides in the hands of a group or of a single person: a king, an emperor, the pope... and this is not so for Sicily. I think that this condition of subjection to different rulers - from the Spaniards to the Piedmontese, the unification of Italy to the Republic - has trained the inhabitants of Sicily to adapt to language and customs, behavior, practices, and even psychological disposition.

Int|AR: Today we have invaders of a different nature. What are the elements that pose the greatest threat to present day Sicily?

RC: Unfortunately it is largely internal invaders. The condition of subjection and millennia of adaptation to colonization have simultaneously developed in Sicilians different aptitudes and skills, both good and bad, and, at times, seemingly contrasting: hospitality towards a stranger as nothing more than a "get rich" scheme, kindness vs. distrust; submission vs. contempt; inferiority vs. arrogance; roughness vs. refinement; generosity as a form of seduction that creates a kind of double bond, a circular one: 'my gift in any way belongs to me'. These qualities and characteristics, at times extreme, distinguish different individuals from delicate to terrible, and can coexist in the same person or the same social groups. For certain, today the Sicilian capacity to adapt is evident from the absence of any form of discrimination, a disposition that certainly comes from mixed social customs and a certain proportion of ethnic hybridization of ancient origins. The adaptation, I think, took place in passing with mistrust, accession, intermarriage, and autodidactic skills. A true exercise of an intermediate ground that urges the attitude to- "take the shape of things".

Many of these interesting and perverse contradictions can explain, I think, the phenomenon of the mafia, proudly separatist and stupidly antiprogressive, bloodthirsty and religious, traditional and unscrupulous, like an invader that is, at the same time, part of an invasive body; and not only as a society, but at times as individuals, though in varying degrees, through deep cultural structures that are stratified within us, like the jarring and fascinating co-presences of our architectures, that like spaceships, seem to come come from different worlds, both near and far.

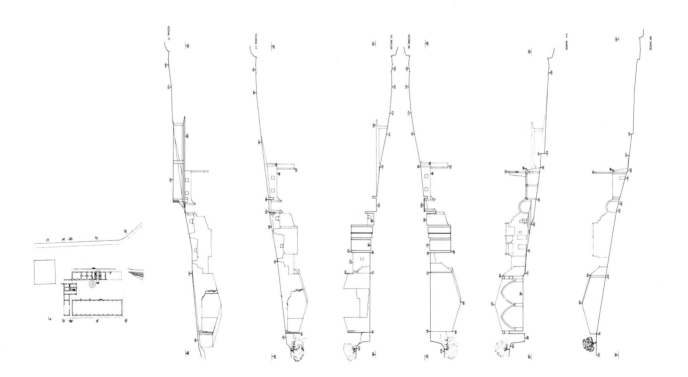

Sections through Case di Stefano, a new museum incorporating the ruins of an old farmhouse destroyed by earthquake, Gibellina

Case di Stefano, Gibellina

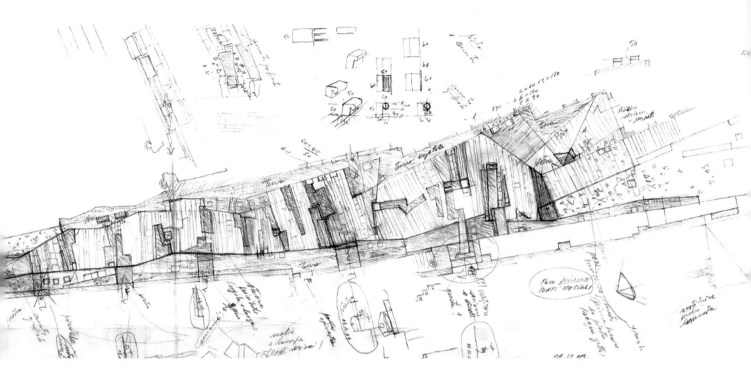

Int|AR: What of Sicily's architectural resilience? Did Sicily's architecture adapt itself to the styles of its many different inhabitants; Greeks, Romans, Normans, Arabs? How did each period adapt to the last to arrive at the coherent whole that is present today in Sicilian cities? What characterizes the present day architecture of Sicily? How does modern day architecture co-exist with the past, both in adaptive reuse projects and in new construction?

RC: The coexistence of architecture from different eras was very natural until the early decades of the last century. But modern thought, with the myth of progress, at first blush has made it seem impossible to accept each hypothetical coexistence, theorizing and urging a certain erasure of the past, replacing it with the 'new'.

In Italy the question of coexistence between modern and historic architecture takes on special characteristics in view of the enormous consistency of our heritage, with a fatal production of false conscience. After the end of the war, an initial period of excessive boldness in confronting the past, characterized by reckless destruction, was followed by the development of a true and proper ideology of preservation that produced devastating and anachronistic para-picturesque forms. It is a matter of two extreme visions, two attitudes placed obtusely in opposition. The need to safeguard the works of the past operationally overturns new construction through mimetic practices-especially in historic city centres - that make them resemble

ancient ones, at times grotesque and always inauthentic. I believe the only way to preserve, in the sense of "passing down the care of the object and its meaning", is to continue to transform it; naturally, the extent of the transformation depends on the object, which in many cases must remain intact, as a precious document of itself for the world, while others ask to be transformed to an adequate extent, if only to survive and continue to have a sense of the old and the current. And this is especially true for architecture and for the city.

A way of being modern or more humbly, adequate to the times, it seems to me is not to necessarily and demonstratively contrast every new building with the past, but to look for forms and conditions specific to each problem, to recognize a sort of DNA to modify it profoundly, if this also gives it a new sense.

Int|AR: The city of Gela is an example of a city that has evolved, for better or worse, since its founding by the Greeks. It has a long history of survival; Roman, Byzantine and Arabic domination, its re-emergence under Federico II, its survival through warfare and its lamentable fate in the modern era with the violence imposed upon it in the 1980's. What defines Gela in the 21st century? Your winning competition entry *una via tre piazze* was a long time in the making. What is the history of the commission? What were the city's goals? What were your goals? How does the design mediate between the historic layers?

Sketch of the winning competition proposal, Gela

RC: I believe Gela is a 20th century hybrid city. It has eighty thousand inhabitants and suffers the typical contradictions of a modernization without growth. At Gela illegal and wild building coexists, the interesting effects of the synergy between "enterprise and culture" and the idea of 'social condition,' theorized by Adriano Olivetti, experimented on the rationalist neighborhood of Macchitella (see website for full discussion on Macchitella).

As for the time for the completion of the first intervention ...? In Sicily, time takes on a metaphysical dimension and actions seem to be independent of their ends. I won the competition in 1993. There were immediate public presentations and enthusiastic reactions. It seemed that everyone wished the projects realized, as soon as possible. In 1998, I was commissioned to do the design of the first intervention, the Piazza Roma, the most complex and interesting part that was tied to the creation of a public building with small shops; there would have been an upper square with a garden and a low one which overlooked a long 'urban room'.

The project was delivered on time but by then, the municipal administration was so fragile that, primarily due to a lack of organization, it did not succeed in getting approved by the municipal Council. Political factions, not necessarily in opposition, provoked these useless and self-destructive incidents.

Finally, in 2000, a strong willed official from the City Planning Office succeeded in getting the entire competition project approved as a general urban project, and beginning the commission from the other square at the opposite end of historic center, that is now realized.

The work began in 2006, but the contractor was not up to the task and it took more time to appoint another. Meanwhile, in 2005, at the behest of the new mayor they entrusted me with the second part of the project: 3/4 of the Corso and the other three piazzas, excluding the Piazza Roma, now definitively compromised.

The new mayor, in fact, a fierce opponent of the competition while he was municipal councilor – purely

Pavement from the realized part of the *Una via tre piazze* competition, Gela

Pavement construction, Gela

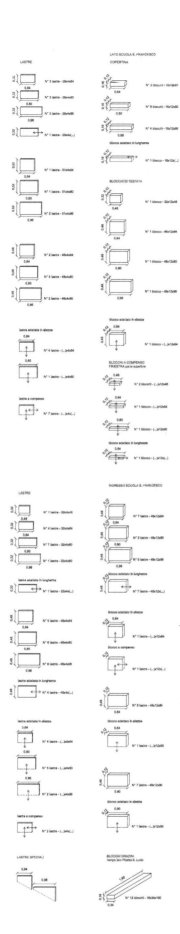

for the sake of political rivalry - as soon as he took office attacked it as he had before, but without succeeding in reviving the dissent of the previous years. So far, my ' 1° Prize ', unanimously selected by a competent and strong jury, has built only a square and a solo section of the Corso; to do this it took about six years. A paradoxical situation!

From time to time, lazy and inefficient civil servants and citizen groups opposed to any transformation have thought to slow down the second part of the project. The executive project was approved more than two years after the other four due to a stretch bristling with obstacles and boycotts. Up to now, the administration has not taken any effective financing initiative-about 8 million euros-to complete the construction.

The municipal administration had entrusted the architects, organisers of the competition, with the elaboration of the theme; from the wording of the notice, one was aware that the competition was designed to transform public spaces in a modernist direction; it solicited an exercise in design, as there was neither a real program, clear themes nor precise objectives. In the absence of a program, the design of the pavement became almost the only theme, so the risk of an excess of graphics was great.

For my part it was clear right from the beginning that I had to critically face the philosophy of the notice; to bring to life everything that was not said in the notice and the latent and specific question of that area of work and its geographical and urban condition. We worked against any form making and beautification of the historic centre, to some precise urban changes that could start a concrete integration between the degraded historic center, degraded but still of some interest, and the outskirts, the product of wild speculative building, microscopic, widespread and extensive.

Attention to the structure of the urban spaces and the buildings that define them allows one to experiment with forms and relationships laden with new meanings; the areas of my work are naturally the urban trans-formations that face the new needs of the historic city and especially the various relationships with the 'city without qualities' that has grown disproportionately around it.

Int|AR: What threatens cities today and what is necessary in city planning to develop capacities to absorb future shocks and stresses?

RC: The cities today risk a vital and self-destructive chaos of no specific interest, the opposite of rich, cultured and vital chaos that comes from the city's

Pavement unit types at Gela

history. I am skeptical of the urban planning discipline and its ability to predict and plan. Of course I am referring especially to urban planning in Italy. Italy has, I think, the most complex and articulated system of town planning in the world; notwithstanding that it is a country with a high incidence of illegal building and a persistent ineffectiveness. This happens for a collection of reasons: untimeliness, the lack of checks and controls; the complicated rules and practices of approval and authorization, referencing a nineteenth-century bureaucracy; finally the slow processing of plans, their lack of simplicity, an overly long validation in relation to the rapidly changing phenomena of transformation.

Int|AR: One key aspect of resilience theory relates to disaster, disaster recovery and strategies for avoiding disaster. Your projects at Salemi and Gibellina are a direct result of natural disaster, the devastating earthquake of 1968, Terremoto del Belìce. Historically one of western Sicily's largest seismic events, this earthquake destroyed 14 towns including Gibellina and parts of Salemi. Disaster relief was hindered by the lack of preparation, excessive bureaucracy and, as noted in Leonardo Sciascia's January 1968 articles in *L'Ora*, a lack of trust on the part of the refugees of help from outside the island, a result of the social differences between the north and south

of Italy. Do you think these issues have any relevance today?

RC: From the age-old problem of the 'Southern question', which was already present at the end of the 19th century and of which Antonio Gramsci accurately wrote in the '20s, one can say that its results are still visible in the jarring presence of the signs of modernity such as, for example, highways and obvious states of marginalization and neglect, natural beauty and inefficient services. It is a paradox, seeing that Sicily was the first Italian region to have a statute of regional autonomy approved in 1946, a year before the Constitution of the Italian Republic; even if the advanced concessions were the obstacles to the constituent Government and the fragile separatist movement of Finocchiaro Aprile. With respect to the refugees' distrust of State intervention, I can say that it was justly founded.

"...Witness the jarring discrepancy between the state intentions and the local situation, written by Ludovico Corrao, (introduction to the book *I maestri di Gibellina* by Davide Camarrone, for editions Sellerio 2011) in which he tells that the Government of those years had not even raised the issue of reconstruction, to the extent of making available boats to send the families of the earthquake to South America or Australia. Later, in the vision of the State, the issue of Belìce, became

The Belice region after the earthquake, from the exhibition *Belice '80.*

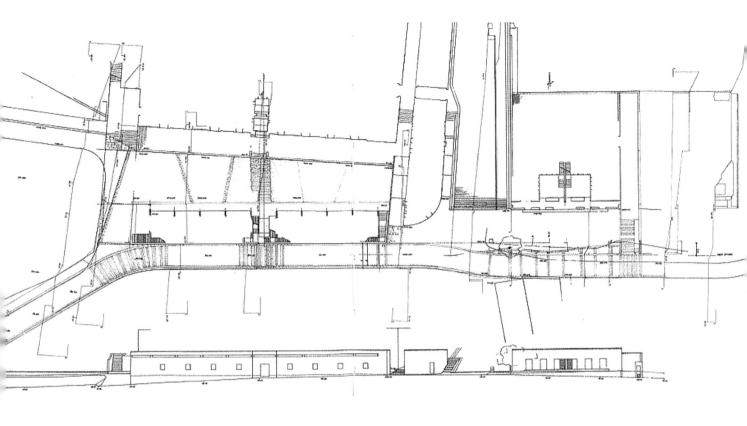

an almost exclusive problem of physical reconstruction and this involved not so much an investment for the construction of new infrastructure, public buildings and homes, as applications of an automatic model, a pure transfer of money without the production of wealth...' (From "Utopia di Gibellina", in Roberto Collovà, *Piccole figure che passano*, "22 publishing" Milano, 2012).

Int|AR: Recovery efforts were extremely slow and took more than a decade to materialize. Your project with Álvaro Siza to rebuild parts of the historic center of Salemi did not take place until the 1980's. What were the reasons for this lengthy delay of recovery efforts?

RC: Immediately after '68 concrete platforms were constructed almost exclusively to accommodate barracks for the earthquake victims. A great deal was demolished, much of it avoidable, in the emotion of the emergency, with the goal of a more consistent reconstruction.

'....The earthquake of 1968 in the Valley of Belìce left ruined a poor but often erudite architecture. With reconstruction, each city gave rise to three cities: the ancient city, at times only in ruins; the shantytown, cement terraces for the installation of prefabricated houses; the new town, built often with an urban model

TOP
Plan, Case di Stefano, Gibellina

BOTTOM
Temporary housing after the earthquake, from the exhibition *Belice '80*.

unsuitable for responding to specific issues and to the complexity of the issues posed by the disaster. The completely destroyed ancient cities had been abandoned. When the destruction was partial it was rebuilt over or next to them. In the shantytown, over time, wood and plates have been replaced or supplemented by new masonry walls; footings and tanks, have improved their functioning with protection against the climate; the individual vegetation began to merge and take on an urban consistency; the slums became resistant and stable for decades, integrated by poor signage and street furniture. Self-organizational processes developed in the shantytown from the '70s to present day have created forms resistance to urban systems and certain essential public and domestic qualities of real places, creating a strong identity.' (from "Utopia di Gibellina", in *Piccole figure che passano*, Roberto Collovà, 22 publishing, Milano ,2012).

Álvaro Siza and I were in charge of the restoration project for the mother church of Salemi in 1982, after the Belìce '80 Workshops, organized by the initiative of Pierluigi Nicolin and a bunch of us young architects who taught at the Faculty of Architecture in Palermo.

In the twelve years that elapsed between the earthquake (1968) and the Workshops (1980), the mother church that had not collapsed but was badly damaged was demolished for the sake of public safety; noone thought that it could be put back safely.

> **Int|AR:** The severe damage to the historic XVII century Chiesa Madre in the Piazza Alicia destroyed its ability to function as a church. It however presented an opportunity for a reuse of the site for a new purpose. The work is twofold; the visible design interventions are often structural and purposefully minimal with a distinct architectural vocabulary while the invisible ones change the urban plan and historic use of Piazza Alicia and the Chiesa Madre.

RC: I would say there are structural interventions both invisible and visible. The construction was very poor, in spite of its erudite architecture; the mortar of the walls was pulverized and the interventions consisted of preventive repair of the external stone walls in 'stone sacks' with the technique of ' stitch and unstitch '; the wall was later injected with cement mortar after having been reinforced with steel bars inserted in a quincunx every 60 cm. Even the operations on the ruins are visible and structural. The walls had been cut at different heights according to their shape and the top of the wall was completed by a band of white limestone blocks, trapped on sheets of lead to protect the cut; final forms showed the anatomical features of the construction, accentuated by interior stucco, now exterior, to reinforce the trans-

TOP
Plan of Piazza Alicia and the Mother Church, Salemi
BOTTOM
Mother Church after the earthquake, Salemi

formation of the Church into a public open space. Other visible changes within the internal perimeter of the Church are sustained by the continuous use of material from the pavement that is of the same white limestone, ' Bush-hammered ' in part from the old town square and cut by a wire ' saw '.

Int|AR: How do the two types of interventions relate to each other? What role do the new materials (steel struts, new paving) play in the new use? Are there any lessons here for seismic interventions to other surrounding buildings for future prevention?

RC: We made a thorough survey of thresholds, stairs, ramps, parapets, cornices, balconies, plates ... by making very precise typological indications for all these minute elements, adapting historical typologies and devising new ones in reference to new requirements, as for example, in making the ground floor of the houses by the steep streets accessible for car parking. The solutions studied are recurring and thus applicable throughout the rest of the historic center, as from a manual. With regard to prevention in relation to seismic events we did not experiment, not so much due to the lack of technological solutions, as to resistant regulations.

To reduce risks and to limit the damages, it sufficed that the stone and wood constructions were made to the

'rule of art'. Many of the collapses in Salemi were due to damage from poor construction often associated with the improper use of reinforced concrete that produce mixed structural systems with inconsistent levels of stiffness; the ability to adapt was diminished and the fragility grew in relation to earthquakes, of course within certain limits.

Int|AR: As an outdoor plaza/ monument how does your design intervention change the historic center with its important position at the top of the hillside and in juxtaposition with the Castello? How does this change in the urban plan impact the future growth and development of the town itself?

RC: This project has given the city a modern square and at the same time it has regenerated the old piazza profiting from the phenomenon of the catastrophic earthquake, like a transforming energy for the future. It has made some new open and semi-public spaces available for leisure and cultural activities as well as for meeting places.

We have done our job. It is now for the Administration to profit from these new possibilities that, in fact, have radically changed the structure and image of the city, without betraying its identity. Now it's just a matter of initiative and organization. By now at Salemi and

Piazza Alicia, the new urban space from the ruins of the Mother Church, Salemi

Gibellina there is even a special tourism from architects and students coming from schools of architecture in Europe and other places, typically, Swiss and German.

Int|AR: While the city has continued to thrive for 45 years since the earthquake, many neighborhoods of Salemi remain ruined as in 1968. The Carmine neighborhood is one such area with many condemned, roofless structures of half walls. Your project with Marcella Aprile and Francesco Venezia, Il Teatro all'aperto del Carmine, is set amongst these ruins. Built on the old footprint of the Carmine convent, the concept of a community garden and an outdoor theater is a healing one. The serene nature of the architecture supports such a program with the backdrop of the valley beyond. However, this poetic space with its amazing views of the Belice region stands vacant, strangled by weeds. What stands in the way of recovery for these areas? How do these damaged areas affect the life of the city itself as it evolves?

RC: I am sorry to continually return to issues of management and politics, but this is the real problem. Unfortunately each Administration tends to ignore

the actions and achievements of the previous. This irresponsible distraction influences the citizens, becomes a true delegitimizing of works that causes them to be unused, scorned, and indirectly reduced to ruin. A self-destructive form of extremely expensive administrative discontinuity. The Sgarbi administration in Salemi not only ignored the value of the new works, (mother church, squares and streets, open-air theater, the Cascio draft plan of the subdivision behind the Church, designed in detail by us but unfulfilled, historic centre of U. Riva) but tended to characterize them as a caricature in the eyes of the citizens, urging a form of vulgarity through somewhat picturesque uses. Once a Secretary of the Sgarbi party said to me with respect to the Teatro del Carmine: ' ... This work is interesting, pity we don't know what to do with it ...', I answered: ' ....make it a theater... just prepare a program, very economically created by the students and teachers of schools ... ' Some time after they waterproofed the central part of the theater, forming a 60 cm deep tub filled with red wine. Dancers in bathing suits went in and out of this pool at a wine tasting. I went to the tasting and I met Sgarbi who was very polite and complimentary: I told him I was very satisfied, if the theater worked well for that scene, then it would work for any other

LEFT
View from the town looking up towards Piazza Alicia

RIGHT
The ruins of the Mother Church as a new urban space

representation, it was truly a theater, it could continue. But nothing happened.

A weak point of the theatre is its isolation; before the project was executed we drafted a masterplan of the Carmine neighborhood, in which the theater is just the first of the interventions. The theatre is among the ruins in the area because you cannot rebuild homes for geological reasons. Therefore the plan assumed, as a guiding concept, the recovery and conversion of each portion of ruins as a typological urban transformation of the neighborhood of Carmine in the park, with the use of the ruins of destroyed houses and estates like an open quarry of naked architectural elements. The lack of realization of the other interventions of the Plan is, together with the absence of a program, the main reason for abandonment and decay.

Int|AR: Your photographs exhibited this past summer at the Museo d'arte contemporanea "Ludovico Corrao" in Gibellina, (*Belice '80*), portray Gibellina, new and old, as it remakes itself after the earthquake. The images capture a spirit of silent endurance and, at times, resignation. What are your thoughts today in looking at these images, so many years after you captured those moments?

RC: During these months I have been working on a new report on the Belìce, after more than thirty years since those black-and-white photographs, with the idea of putting the two stories together. It's hard work, a lot has changed for better or for worse. The countryside has irrevocably changed and, as a result, the new report will produce a different landscape.

For example, in the 80's travel on the highways that were rarely used was like moving in a low flight over the territory, the highway almost disappeared and one perceived a poor but essential country, with isolated farms-like the Case Di Stefano; one saw small homes and "pagghiari", the agricultural warehouses consisting of only one very small room. Now, along the highways, huge eucalyptus trees impede the view of that countryside now, consolidated in memory, and compel one's attention of the stretch as a blind corridor.

Int|AR: In *Il Gattopardo* (The Leopard), Tomasi di Lampedusa's famed novel of Sicily in the Risorgimento, Tancredi, the last in a line of nobility, says "Se vogliamo che tutto rimanga come è, bisogna che tutto cambi." (If we want everything to remain as is, everything must change.) Sicily has changed

TOP
Interventions behind the Mother Church, Salemi

BOTTOM
Plan at the pergola adjacent to the Mother Church, Salemi

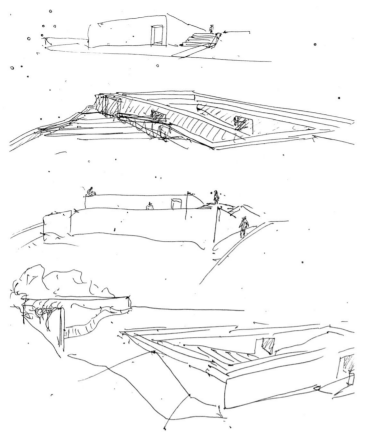

themselves to an essential production and even more refined fare instead of importing almost everything from Trapani including bread, vegetables and fruits, as they do now, waiting to sell everything at a higher price to tourists for two months of the year. It is possible that they will plant fruit orchards and engage in organic farming and then everything remains as it is, indeed, one can conserve development while improving the environment. Would this hypothesis be a fascinating form of resilience? But the new buyers, for their part, seem to want to use the forty hectares of land around il Baglio to plant a large vineyard, just as the Florios had done. And it is presumably that, in addition to vineyards there will be vegetable gardens and orchards and maybe even olive trees. And one can't exclude the possibility that this production would immediately have a brand.

Then Levanzo could transform itself into a kind of medieval castle, a little kingdom, where the inhabitants, like those of the villages at the foot of the Castle, will have to orient their attitudes towards the needs of the new rulers and return to being farmers and fishermen, but in service? Would this less fascinating hypothesis be a form of resilience?

dramatically in the last decade with development of the coastal towns for tourism - for example, the arrival of Prada on one of the remote Egadi islands. Is this necessary for Sicily to remain as it is?

RC: I imagine you refer to the island of Levanzo, a delightful place where I go on vacation once or twice a year. Prada has solely aquired a beautiful and large house in the centre of Cala Dogana and il Baglio, property of the Florio family, on the plateau above the village. I don't think there is any intention of producing one of their boutiques on the island as it would be the end of one's holidays with friends. However this recent event could solicit some interesting reflections on the life of the inhabitants of Levanzo, on the tourists that frequent the place, though almost exclusively in July and August, on the economy of the island, but also on some likely curious denials of tardy, progressive ideas of history in the globalized post-modern world. The economy provided by new visitors seems certainly stronger than that of the approximately 226 inhabitants of the island, two thirds of whom, on the other hand, winter in Trapani. The prospect, in its anachronism, could be of great interest ... say ... ecologically: the fish are not wanting, it is possible that the inhabitants are pushed to dedicate

TOP
Sketches of open air theater, Salemi

BOTTOM
Open air theater, Carmine neighborhood, Salemi

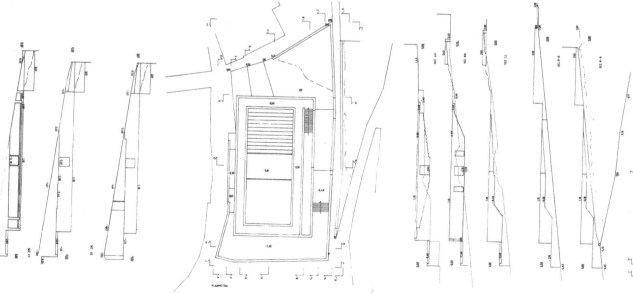

TOP
View looking through open air theater, Salemi

BOTTOM
Sections through open air theater, Salemi

Roberto Collovà is an Italian architect whose expansive body of work includes urban design, landscape design, furniture and photography. He is the author of *Piccole figure che passano*. He also writes for different journals in Italy and elsewhere. He has taught at the Facoltà di Architettura di Palermo and at the Academia di Architettura of Mendrisio in Switzerland as well as in institutions that include Barcelona, Lisbon, Las Palmas, Venice.

His work was exhibited at the Venice Biennale and the Milan Triennale. His many awards include the Premio IN_ARCH for Design, the Premio Gubbio for architecture in historic centers, finalists in the Mies van der Rohe Award in 1990, finalist in the Italian Architectural Gold Medal Award 2003, winner of the Competition internazionale Diagonal, Barcellona 1989, winner of the Competition *Una via, tre piazza*, Gela 1993, winner of the Competition for the Masterplan at S. Cesarea Terme 2007.

He was on the jury for the Mies van der Rohe Award 2005, BSI Swiss Architectural Award 2008 and for the Young Architects Program MAXXI / MoMa Ps 2011-2013. He lives and works in Palermo, Sicily.

The Belice region after the earthquake, from the exhibition *Belice '80*

BEIT BEIRUT

RECONSTRUCTION & THE TRACES OF WAR

by DANA HAMDAN

Crisis can be defined as a worsening set of conditions, immediate or foreseen, with various scales of physical or perceived impact. It can be a large uncontrollable force of nature (e.g. earthquakes, floods), a hybrid of natural force and human action (e.g. fires), or deliberate human will (e.g. conquering armies, aerial bombardment, terrorist strikes). Confronting crisis, resilience is the ability to react, recover, and resist. Through psychological coping mechanisms human beings can re-establish normal equilibrium when threatened by adverse circumstances. In a parallel manner, buildings can also be resurrected in the wake of abandonment and ruin. An analogy can be drawn between psychological mechanisms of recovery and architectural strategies dealing with devastated environments.

In 1975 a sectarian civil war erupted in Lebanon to end 15 years later. The city of Beirut was most affected by this crisis, with hundreds of thousands of people dead and many neighborhoods brought to ruin. Today, only a few punctured buildings bearing the scars of war remain standing. This makes the reconstruction process seem successful at first blush, but in fact it only outwardly erased and embellished the scars, and left the Lebanese society deeply fractured. The fifteen-year internal conflict was a brutal war that resulted in a collective trauma, leading the Lebanese to question their national identity. Confronting this post-traumatic calamity, with reminders most recently by the fighting in the northern city Tripoli at the Syrian borders, Lebanese today still need to embrace their resilience.

Human Psychology
In his article "Loss, Trauma, and Human Resilience," George Bonanno defined resilience as the ability to maintain a state of normal equilibrium in the face of extreme, adverse circumstances. He proclaims that the pathway to resilience would be through understanding the determinants of the traumatic memory. The deeper the understanding and the healthier the remembrance, the more resilience is enhanced. He suggested various schemes to achieve such an outcome, which

New extension linking two wings of existing house

included coping strategies and attitudes that show insight, initiative, optimism, creativity and even humor[1].

Contrastingly, some resort to nostalgia in the face of a traumatic situation. Nostalgia is a powerful emotion that can blind one from objectively reflecting on the past. Andrew Beckerman wrote in the review of the film *Nostalgia for the Light*, " Nostalgia essentially derives its force from a false remembrance of history. Nostalgia, the longing to return home, is never about a real home, but an idealized one, flushed of the nuances."[2] It is a painful melancholic feeling that keeps a person dreaming of a glorified past that (might) have existed one day. Nostalgia in the face of trauma is thus a disruption to the process of understanding its determinants, and henceforth a disruption to resilience.

People can also experience amnesia during psychological trauma. By definition, it is a deficit in memory caused by brain damage, disease, or also psychological trauma. By the same token, it interferes with the ability to grasp the traumatic experience, and in its turn, deranges the process of resilience.

Architecture and the Psychological Analogy

In the context of the built environment, Thomas J. Campanella argues that "any study of the city in history will reveal that human settlements possess an essential ability to resurrect themselves in the wake of devastation."[3] Buildings are traces of the past, and a doorway to understanding history, traumatic history before all else; they can, but more so, should be saved and reused after they have been led to decay. An analogy can be drawn between architecture and the above mentioned psychological explanation of trauma and mechanisms of recovery; Adaptive Reuse[4] of buildings can thus be viewed and should be considered as the architectural pathway to the resilience of cities that have been impacted by crisis, in Beirut's case, by ravaging war. Nostalgia too has an analogous strategy in architecture. It is the restorative attempt that draws upon past images through remaking tactics that "preserve" a desired form and function. Similarly, amnesia would be the oblivious demolition of buildings to build anew.

Beit Beirut & Post War Reconstruction

Applying the above analogy, a path to Lebanese national resilience may be attainable through architecture, and, in particular, through the Adaptive Reuse strategy that saves buildings from amnesiac demolition and nostalgic restoration.

When war came to rest in 1990 the Lebanese community seemed to have a consensual agreement to immediately begin reconstruction, while the governmental body of the state of Lebanon itself was in need of restructuring. Consequently, private real estate companies were created and entrusted with the implementation of reconstruction works, the promotion, marketing, and sale of properties to individuals or developers[5]. This implied that the role of the government as a civic body was negligible in the reconstruction process, with the decision-making often in the hands of private developers, whose priorities were to maximize profits and "to construct modern structures that would compete in the

Beit Bakarat, the intersection of Independence Street and Damascus Road

global markets."[6] Heated debates would occasionally occur between those developers and property owners, intellectuals, historians, social scientists, urban planners and architects, strong believers that buildings play a powerful societal role. As a result, a few buildings were sporadically selected to be preserved for their "historical values," but numerous other sites were erased with the promise to rebuild while remaining faithful to the urban fabric[7]. Unfortunately most of the time it resulted in either pure facadism, extending from what used to exist, or construction entirely new and alien to the context. The preservation process, when it happened, was questionable as it failed to ensure continuity of character, reconciliation, and resilience. Hashim Sarkis attributes that to the war itself; while in the 1970s other cities were busy discussing how preservation strategies could address intangible social dimensions, Beirut, Lebanon, was plunged into its internal war[8].

Of the many nostalgic restorations, the Artisan's House is one and non-exclusive example of how structures were often superficially remodeled to a supposed "traditional Lebanese character" of the far past, ignoring an entire era of pre-war trendsetting and innovative local modernism.

As for the equally numerous amnesiac demolitions, the Carlton Hotel, an architectural asset of the heyday of 1950s modernism, is one of the most infamous examples. In 2008, a real estate Lebanese company launched a competition to replace the Carlton with a high-end residential program. In the promotion for his "perfect on every level" proposal, the developer recalls the successful days of the Carlton[9]. However, the decision was made to demolish the building and replace it with a high-rise "modern" tower despite the many adaptive reuse schemes that were presented.

With its nonconformance to nostalgic and amnesiac trends of reconstruction that prevailed post war, Beit Beirut is one of the few examples of a conscious preservation. It not only saves a demarcation line heritage building from destruction, but also retrofits its program and design to include a war memorial program that will help the Lebanese face and reconcile their painful past.

Beit Beirut[10], previously known as Beit Barakat, is one of Beirut's most beautiful yellow sandstone buildings[11] . Its importance comes from its clever architecture and its crucial location at the intersection of Independence Street (Elias Sarkis Avenue) and Damascus Road, the site of the war time demarcation line dividing the city into two camps. It was built as the residence of the Barakat family by architects Youssef Aftimos and Fouad Kozah in 1924, and 1932, an example of the transition between early sandstone building techniques and later building trends that came with the introduction of concrete as a building material[12]. In that period when the main living room, or salon, the most important

part of the home, occupied the corner position of corner buildings, one of the most important architectural features in Beit Barakat was the placement of a central void at the corner of the intersection. This void brought light to the interior and allowed every other room of the house transparency and visual connection with the streets of the city.

Unfortunately, militiamen benefitted from this architecture, and transformed the building into a war machine in 1975. In the context of war the corner void was the perfect location for a sniper's hideout. The magnificent visual axis that was intended to provide visual

Light material such as glass and mirrors in the addition anchor and emphasize the presence of the original structure as a place where "no sniper would dare settle in."

transparency within the building became a line of death through which snipers aimed at their targets. Room after room they built their barricades of stacked sand and concrete walls, with rectangular openings, culminating in a funnel-shaped shooting range; an arrangement that allowed the snipers to aim at their targets from the safety of the back room. With its bullet-riddled facades, this building became a symbol of the civil war to many Lebanese.

In 1997, architect and preservation activist Mona Hallak succeeded in staying a demolition process that would have taken this house down. She launched a campaign to urge the municipality of Beirut to expropriate the building for a museum for the memory of the city. She finally succeeded in 2003[13]. The building is now undergoing reconstruction, and is expected to open to the public in 2015. The decision was made to transform the building into a cultural and urban documentation center that will shed light on the memories of the city after the Ottoman period. It aims to create a collective

memory that would heal the divisions within the fractured post-war Lebanese society.

The architect's strategy of intervention is two-fold. The restoration of the original building renders it solid and weatherproof, retaining the scars of war. This preservation of its brokenness with an affective physical presence evokes feelings of regret. A new addition in the form of a contemporary architectural extension links the two corner wings of the existing house. Light material such as glass and mirrors will both anchor and emphasize the presence of the original structure as a place where "no sniper would dare settle in", according to the reconstruction architect Youssef Haidar[14]. It will be a place for the Lebanese to contemplate and reflect as they try to grasp the consequences of war.

The first floor will be dedicated to artifacts and symbols of the war years that were found in situ. The restoration scheme preserves the snipers' war architecture of 1.8 meter deep barricade walls, the narrow slits through which they fired their guns, and the graffiti

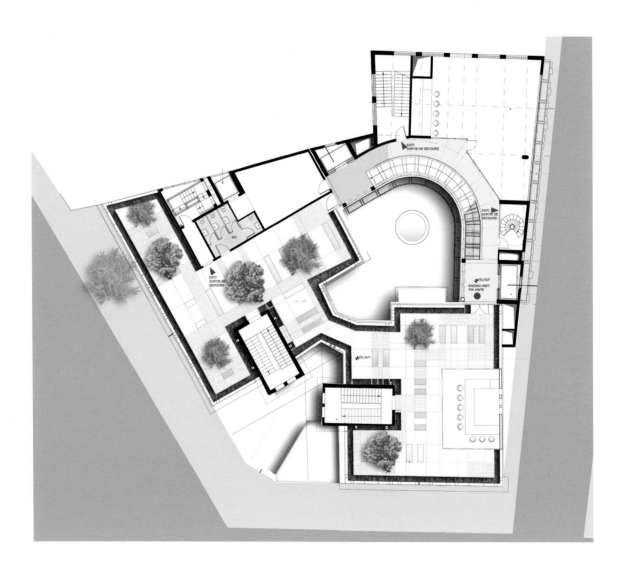

Top floor plan of reconstruction and extension

covering the wall with signatures of snipers and war quotes. These atrocious marks of war will not be erased, but will instead be part of the permanent museum of memory as a reminder to the Lebanese of a near potential fate. The second floor will focus on the modern history of Beirut and the third floor will be dedicated to temporary exhibitions and a rooftop garden[15]. Although the new program adopted in this building chiefly makes of it a war memorial, it is the architectural strategy itself that will truly convey the vanity of war.

Many tactics adopted in Beirut's post-war reconstruction did not properly address the past. Most of them shirked from admitting the atrocities of war. Instead, there was spatial erasure and neglect, or the nostalgic attempts to remake as a means to fit "the Lebanese identity". These strategies that failed in implementing adaptive reuse, also failed in achieving resilience. The vision for Beit Beirut however is an optimistic one. By preserving the traces of war, and introducing a space for remembrance, Beit Beirut hopes to become a much needed place of national healing and unity.

ENDNOTES:

1 Bonanno, G.A. "Loss, Trauma, and Human Resilience: have we underestimated the human capacity to thrive after extremely aversive events?" *American Journal of Psychology*; 59, 2004. P. 20-28

2 Andrew Beckerman to Film-Forward Review online forum, March 18, 2011, *Nostalgia for the light,* http://film-forward.com/nostalgia.html

3 Thomas Campanella, "September 11th and the City," The Resilient City (blog), http://web.mit.edu/dusp/resilientcity/second_level/Topics.html

4 Adaptive Reuse is defined by the Rhode Island School of Design's Department of Interior Architecture journal *Int/AR* as the field that "includes the reuse of existing structures and materials, transformative interventions, continuation of cultural phenomena, connections across the fabric of time and space, and preservation of memory."

5 Salam, Assem, 'The Role of Government in Shaping the Built Environment', in *Projecting Beirut: Episodes in the Construction and Reconstruction of a Modern City*, ed. Peter Rowe and Hashim Sarkis (Munich, London and New York: Prestel 1998), pp. 131.

6 Aseel Sawalha, *Reconstruction Beirut: Memory and Space in a Postwar Arab City,* (Austin: University of Texas Press, 2010), 48.

7 Assem Salam, 'The Role of Government in Shaping the Built Environment', *Projecting Beirut: Episodes in the Construction and Reconstruction of a Modern City* (Munich, London, New York: Prestel, 1998), p. 132.

8 Sarkis, Hashim, "Beirut, Beirut," *The Resilient City Colloquium*, Lecture, Web,

9 http://www.jamilibrahim.com.lb/current.php : "The 5-star Carlton hotel was once the most illustrious landmark and celebrity hot spot of the region. Host to countless upscale events, it became home to affluent dignitaries and the crème de la crème. International media magnates such as royal families, political figures and movie stars partook in glorious festivities and ambiance that the hotel had to offer. As a tribute to a nostalgic era and a vision towards the new rise of excellence, Jamil Ibrahim Est. offers luxury seeking patrons the opportunity to live in one of Beirut's historical backdrops."

10 Beit means house in Arabic, the native language of Lebanese.

11 Yellow stone is the reason why the building is also known as Yellow House.

12 Hallak, "Hallak on 'Beit Beirut'," December 08, 2012, DOI: www.theplanisphere.com

According to activist architect Mona Hallak, Aftimos built the first two floors. 8 years later, Aftimos was very busy and the owners desired an addition and for that resorted to Kozah who was fascinated with concrete as a new building material. This gives the building an added value as it becomes an archive on its own of the transition in building techniques.

13 Wheeler, William. "Is Beirut Ready For a Memory Museum Yet?" *The Daily Star Lebanon*, September 14, 2007. http://www.dailystar.com.lb/News/Local-News/Sep/14/Is-Beirut-ready-for-a-memory-museum-yet.ashx#axzz2JYKhwFqA

14 Snaije, Olivia. "From Beit Barakat To Beit Beirut" *The Daily Star Lebanon*, October 01, 2011. http://www.dailystar.com.lb/Culture/Art/2011/Oct-01/150175-from-beit-barakat-to-beit-beirut.ashx#ixzz2JZbalpox

15 Mahdawi, Dalila. "Sodeco' War-Weary Barakat Building To Be Renovated" *The Daily Star Lebanon*, October 02, 2010. http://www.dailystar.com.lb/News/Local-News/Jun/02/Sodecos-war-weary-Barakat-building-to-be-renovated.ashx#axzz2fgE0EtX7

The snipers' lair

TYPOLOGY IN CRISIS
THE REUSE OF COOLING TOWERS

by BIE PLEVOETS & LORE MELLEMANS

Cooling towers are victims of their own scale. Being very large structures, they are the most visible and eye-catching constructions of a nuclear plant. As such the cooling tower has become a symbol, or even icon for nuclear energy. The recent disaster in the Fukushima nuclear plants has strengthened the distrust in and reaction against nuclear power. Popular culture has contributed to the negative position towards this type of building as people associate not only the structure itself with nuclear power but also confuse the emitted 'smoke' with pollution. This is a very common misconception since a cooling tower can only emit water vapor. These structures are also used in other power producing in-dustries and appear on industrial sites of various kinds that provide their own electricity.

In contrast to this poor reputation, these structures are intrinsically ecological as they cool water through a natural draught of air. Moreover, cooling towers of the hyperboloid type, the most common type, are very strong and need little restoration and maintenance[1]. Visually and spatially they also impress as landmarks in urban and rural contexts, and their sublime interiors have the ability to astonish the rare visitor.

With the growth of alternative energy sources, nucear plants and other combustion power plants will start to disappear, and the towers, with the loss of function, are in danger of being torn down. In the Netherlands, where the first hyperboloid cooling towers were constructed in 1917, towers have already been demolished in 1985, even with the status of protected monument since 1970[2]. Unfortunately, this

Cooling Tower IM
Photograph by Isabelle Van Assche

Cooling Tower Petit Maison
Photograph by Isabelle Van Assche

is not an exceptional situation, as documented by the photographers Bernd and Hilla Becher who have made a visual study of cooling towers. Their series of photographs are "urban explorations", a recent trend in photography that brings man-made structures, usually abandoned ruins and neglected buildings, under scrutiny by documenting them for their specific visual qualities and registering their ongoing decay. The Bechers' images show how cooling towers evolved to their present geometric form from 1964 to 1993. In several cases their pictures remain the only witness of this disappearing typology"[3].

Hyperboloid towers: a sustainable construction

The most common geometry of this extraordinary typology is the hyperboloid type, invented in 1917 by the Dutch engineer Frederik Karel Theodoor Van Iterson (1877-1957). This concrete construction replaced early cylindrical wooden typologies[4]. The first hyperbolic concrete cooling tower with its new and innovative concept was constructed in 1917 at the Dutch state coal mine in Heerlen. The shape of the shell is the result of the intention to use straight linear reinforcements, but the complexity of its overall shape was such that Van Iterson could not find an engineering company willing to construct the tower. Finally it was engineer G. Kuypers who accepted the job, executed the works and patented the design in 1916[5].

Van Iterson made his cooling towers based on the laws of nature. The walls are very thin, comparable to the shell of an egg that derives its strength from the curvature of its entire shell. Its geometry enlarges the natural draught, caused by the openings at the base of the tower. The plume we see rising from these towers, approximately only one to two percent of the water that passes through this tower, is only water vapor contrary to popular belief that these are chemical or harmful fumes.

Inspiring shapes

The hyperboloid geometry as developed by Van Iterson is not only an excellent piece of engineering but is also a remarkable architectural form that has inspired many designers.

The first work of architecture in the form of a hyperboloid was designed by the Russian engineer Vladimir Grigorievich Shukhov (1853-1939) as a water tower for the occasion of the 1896 Russian industrial and art exhibition in Nizhniy Novgorod. At that time, the construction was still a lattice steel structure without a solid shell. Shukhov patented his invention and developed numerous structures, such as a radio tower, lighthouses, masts of warships and supports for power transmission lines.

Around the same period, Antoni Gaudi (1852-1926) experimented with hyperboloid shapes in his design for the Sagrada Familia. He used the geometry in the interior of the building, more specifically in the ceiling between the columns supporting the roof. Gaudi used this particular shape to bring natural light into the building while allowing the construction to bear the full load of the building[6].

Once the hyperboloid could be constructed as a solid concrete shell, the shape was used by many architects including Oscar Niemeyer (1907-2012) and Le Corbusier (1887-1965). Niemeyer designed and constructed in 1959 a cathedral for the newly developed city Brasilia in a hyperboloid geometry that would become a landmark for the city[7]. In 1978, he again applied the same geometry in his design for the cultural centre 'Le Volcan' in Le Havre in a much more solid approach[8]. In the work of Le Corbusier the hyperboloid appears on the roof of the "palace of assembly" in Chandigarh, India, again acting as a landmark for the modern city[9].

Reuse of Cooling towers: Status questions

Only a few examples of reusing cooling towers are known. A recurring scenario is the use of the outer shell as a canvas on which images are painted or projected. A famous project is the painting of the Orlando cooling towers in Soweto, South Africa, in 2010 for the occasion of the FIFA World Cup. One of the towers was used as a gigantic billboard and painted with the name and logo of the sponsor; the other tower had colorful paintings representing aspects of the African culture and tradition[10]. This example inspired other projects in South Africa and beyond, even for nuclear plants still in use. In Cruas, France, artist Jean-Marie Pierret painted the surface of the cooling towers in order to improve the public opinion about the plant[11]. A similar but temporary project was realized in Gösgen, Switzerland, with projected natural images such as penguins and butterflies[12]. During the Second World War, cooling towers were 'camouflaged' by artists who with their art blended the enormous structures into the environment in order to make them less of a target[13].

Other examples for reuse, using the impressive height and width of the towers as an essential basis of their new function, are extreme sports and recreational activities. The aforementioned Orlando towers in Soweto are used for base jumping, bungee jumping, climbing, free fall and paintball, and in Meppen, Germany, a cooling tower has been converted into an amusement park attraction[14]. With the exception of sporting activities and amusement attractions, all other known examples for the reuse of cooling towers are limited to the visual effect of the exterior structure. The qualities and potential for reusing the interior of these vast structures have not yet been explored.

An interior approach towards reuse of a cooling tower

One of the main difficulties in reusing a cooling tower is the low adaptability of the structural part of the tower. Perforating the structure in any way would weaken

the structure significantly as the construction derives its strength through the entire shell. A search for new functions for this structure is limited to programs that do not need lateral light and views to the outside.

A student in the Universiteit Hasselt investigated the potential for adaptive reuse of this typology in a design project on a hyperboloid cooling tower from 1952 at a site in Beringen, Belgium. This former important coal site was closed in 1989 and was protected as a national monument six years later. The site will be transformed into a commercial and cultural centre, yet the cooling tower was not included in the current masterplan.

Unlike other examples of reused cooling towers, the concept grew from the interior of the tower, exploiting the contrast between the lower part of the structure and the spacious qualities of the space above. Because of its specific geometry and the hard surfaces of its construction, a cooling tower has a specific acoustic quality, suggesting a performance hall as a new program. Trends towards an experience economy, very evident in the retail sector all over the world, are also emerging in the cultural field[15]. Many artists perform on exclusive locations and in unusual spaces to make their performance a unique and unforgettable experience.

The Round House in London, the Drill Hall of the Park Avenue Armory in New York and the "Gashouder" in Amsterdam are just some examples of such spaces.

To facilitate a performance space in the cooling tower in Beringen, two levels were created. The original openings in the base of the tower are used to create an entrance and the packing (the structural system that keeps the water evenly distributed as it falls through the tower[16]) on the lower level is transformed into a foyer. As this structure is completely made out of concrete, it serves as the support for the upper level where a stage is created. In contrast to the rather dark and intimate atmosphere of the lower level, the stage would open up to the impressive view to the top of the tower. Like a contemporary oculus of a new Pantheon, the opening above will draw the visitor's eye to the top of the tower.

The intention of this particular design project for the cooling tower in Beringen was not to create a ready-to-build plan but to investigate the possibilities for reuse and adaptation of the interior space of such a construction. Such research and design projects could bring cooling towers as a typology under the attention of designers, conservators, policymakers and, eventually, the public at large in Flanders and abroad.

Satsop Nuclear Power Plant, WA
Photograph by Heekyung Kim

ENDNOTES:

1 Lambert-Vancoppenolle Architects (2010). *Restauratie en her-bestemming mijngebouwen site Beringen: voorstudie koeltoren.* (unpublished)

2 Interview with Bernard Lambert, manager of Lambert-Van-coppenolle Architects and specialist in restoration and reuse of industrial buildings, 5 July 2013.

3 Klein, W. *Portraits of Contemporary Photographers Vol.3.* (Documentary, 2000) Accessed 27 April, 2013,

http://www.youtube.com.watch?v=6ZSLvFY1X6g

4 Baker, Donald. *Cooling Tower Performance*. New York: Chemical Publishing, 1984.

5 Lambert-Vancoppenolle Architects, 2010. *Restauratie en her-bestemming mijngebouwen site Beringen: voorstudie koeltoren.* (unpublished)

6 Sagrada Familia. *Hyperboloid*. Accessed 18 April, 2013, http://www.sagradafamilia.cat/sf-eng/docs_instit/geometria3.php

7 Mullaney. *Brasilia* (2011). Accessed 20 April, 2013, http://toknowthyself.files.wordpress.com/2011/01/brasiliacathe-dral01.jpg

8 Levolcan. *Histoire* (2013). Accessed 21 April, 2013, http://www.levolcan.com/le-volcan/histoire

9 Metcalf, T. *AD Classics: Palace of the Assembly/ Le Corbusier* (2011). Accessed 2 May, 2013, http://www.archdaily.com/155922/ad-classics-palace-of-the-assembly-le-corbusier/

10 Orlandotowers. *Orlando towers* (2010). Accessed 4 April, 2013, http://www.orlandotowers.co.za/index.html

11 Environmentalgraffiti. *Mindblowing cooling tower graffiti* (2010). Accessed 4 April, 2013,

http://www.environmentalgraffiti.com/graffiti/news-graffiti-cool-ing-towers-whole-new-perspective-nuclear

12 *Kkg. Kernkraftwerk Gösgen* (2013). Accessed 4 April, 2013, http://www.kkg.ch/fr/i/intro.html

13 Blogspot. *Nuclear coverup: 10 cool examples of cooling tower art* (2011). Accessed 7 March, 2013, http://copyplease.blogspot.be/2011/02/nuclear-coverup-10-cool-examples-of_26.html

14 *Fisser. Millionenprojekt in Meppen: Investor kündigt Startschuss für Freizeitpark an* (2012). Accessed 4 April, 2013, http://www.noz.de/deutschland-und-welt/politik/nieder-sachsen/60499470/millionenprojekt-in-meppen-investor-kuen-digt-startschuss-fuer-freizeitpark-an.

15 Petermans, Ann. "Retail Design in the Experience Economy: Conceptualizing and 'Measuring' Customer Experiences in Retail Environments." Hasselt University & PHL University College, 2012.

16 gc3, http://www.gc3.com, Glossary of Cooling Tower Terms, accessed 10 January 2014

LIVING FUEL

THE INTERIM LINEAR CITY

In an era defined by a global quest for renewable energy and sustainable sources, this project proposes a solution for unprecedented rapid urbanization through the possibilities of nuclear waste.

by EMILY YEUNG

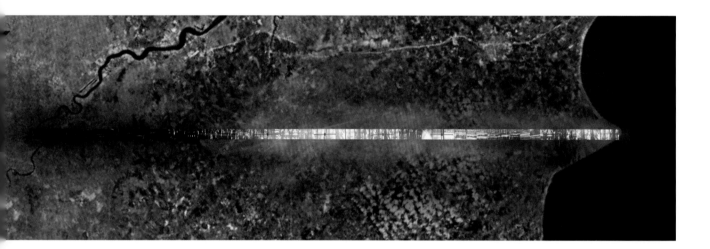

Radioactive waste as energy source

The Magnox nuclear power reactor was once regarded as the zenith of nuclear technology. Widely exported to other countries from the UK as power plants in the 1960's-70's, the Magnox nuclear system is now rendered obsolete by its newer hydroelectric-powered counterparts. Britain's 11[1]Magnox nuclear power stations are currently being decommissioned in a phased program over the next 50 years[2]. The decommissioning involves a 'safe store' strategy[3], established by the HSE HM Nuclear Installations Inspectorate, to remove the radioactive nuclear waste. Guidelines mandate the onsite storage of the buildings containing this waste for 130 years after the station's decommission. Carried out in 3 stages, work commences 30 years after the station's defueling to secure the building structure so that it serves for 100 years as a safe store to contain the radioactive waste until it is safe to remove.

In the first year of shutdown, the residual heat from the stored waste amounts to 31.2MW[4] of energy, and has the potential to power over 20,000[5] households in the first year of the station's decommissioning. The heat is generated by the continuous decay of nuclear fission products after its shutdown. At the 3yr decay mark the residual heat is approximately 2KW per tonne of fuel and equates to 816.52 KW of thermal energy from residual heat[6].

Over time, an exponential decay of heat from the stored waste will occur, stabilizing to approximately 89.5KW at 150 years. If phased correctly, the continuous decommissioning of nuclear stations will provide an uninterrupted energy source that could potentially last hundreds of years.

Crudely speaking, the residual heat emitted by this stored nuclear waste can be converted into usable electricity. The immense thermal energy and long half-life of the nuclear waste could take over a hundred years to cool down. This high level of heat creates a significant temperature difference with its ambient surrounding, which can be used to generate electricity. Recent technological developments in 2013 have produced a new, ionic liquid-based thermocell that "is based on harnessing the thermal energy from the difference in temperature between two surfaces and converting that energy into electricity."[7] This technology is capable of generating electricity with greater efficiency from low-grade steam and converting it into usable energy with no recorded carbon emissions.

This speculation is made possible by the potential of ceramic superconductors[8]. The UK's current electricity network relies on a grid of metal cables. The conductive property of metals, however, causes an energy loss of over 7%[9] of electricity from power station to the household plug. In contrast, extreme cold temperatures generate magnetic fields in ceramics, allowing it to conduct electricity without losing any energy when cooled at the right temperature. This technology creates the potential to produce an efficient electrical power transmission, to minimize energy loss, and to transport across vast distances through thin, lightweight ceramic cables. This material also introduces the potential to create power storage devices, however this currently remains as early stage untested technology.

The Linear City
The Linear City is a proposal to use the residual heat produced by redundant nuclear waste from

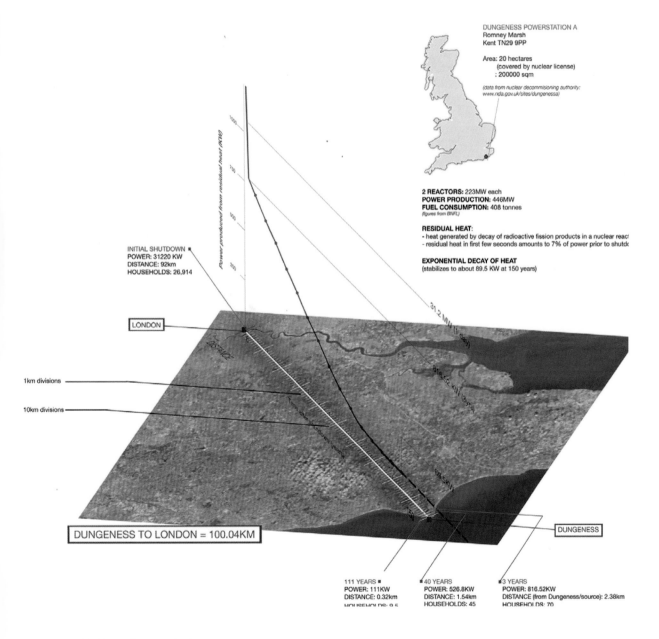

DUNGENESS POWERSTATION A
Romney Marsh
Kent TN29 9PP

Area: 20 hectares
(covered by nuclear license)
: 200000 sqm

(data from nuclear decommissioning authority: www.nda.gov.uk/sites/dungenessa)

2 REACTORS: 223MW each
POWER PRODUCTION: 446MW
FUEL CONSUMPTION: 408 tonnes
(figures from BNFL)

RESIDUAL HEAT:
- heat generated by decay of radioactive fission products in a nuclear react
- residual heat in first few seconds amounts to 7% of power prior to shutd

EXPONENTIAL DECAY OF HEAT
(stabilizes to about 89.5 KW at 150 years)

INITIAL SHUTDOWN
POWER: 31220 KW
DISTANCE: 92km
HOUSEHOLDS: 26,914

LONDON

1km divisions
10km divisions

DUNGENESS TO LONDON = 100.04KM

DUNGENESS

111 YEARS
POWER: 111KW
DISTANCE: 0.32km
HOUSEHOLDS: 9.5

40 YEARS
POWER: 526.8KW
DISTANCE: 1.54km
HOUSEHOLDS: 45

3 YEARS
POWER: 816.52KW
DISTANCE (from Dungeness/source): 2.38km
HOUSEHOLDS: 70

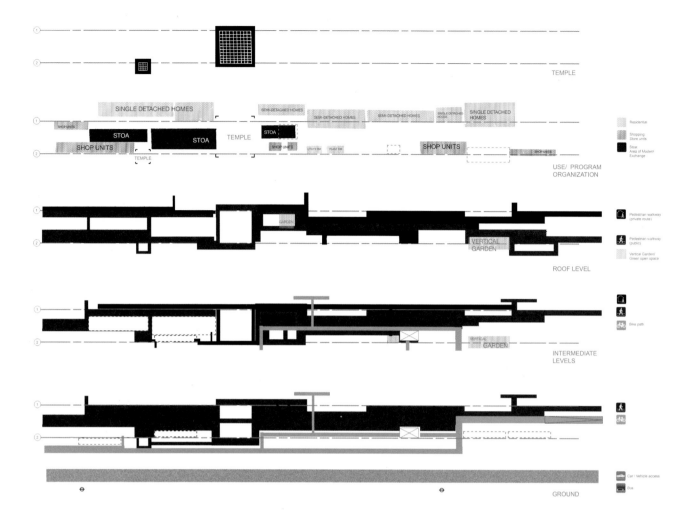

TEMPLE

USE/ PROGRAM ORGANIZATION

ROOF LEVEL

INTERMEDIATE LEVELS

GROUND

decommissioned nuclear power stations as a clean free energy source for modern living. The project proposes the application of super-conducting ceramic cables to transport the energy as direct lines towards London from the abandoned nuclear sites, typically located in satellite coastal towns in the UK. Developing linear links to these potentially abandoned satellite towns allows us to expand our city and to technologically reconnect and develop these areas. The proposed prototype reuses Dungeness Station A, the first Magnox nuclear power station connected to the UK national grid in 1965. The linear city strikes a line as the crow flies running from Dungeness Power Station A to London, expressed as both housing and a transport link.

A masterplan strategy is expressed as an interim linear city capable of growth and adaptation through units constructed from a kit of parts and powered by a high performance ceramic super-conductor smart grid. The linear city can be expanded and adapted along a gridded modular system to cater for other decommissioned sites growing from London.

The System

The linear city is a colonnaded link system guided by a wall of LCD screens. Incorporating housing, transport, and a glazed walkway it is interlaced with the modern temple, vertical wall gardens and retail units. It expands along units of a 5x5m grid and is further subdivided into 1x1m grids where required. Below ground infrastructure contains a high performance smart grid, fibre-optic digital broadband, water and future utilities. Super-conducting ceramic cables will be used as direct energy lines to fuel London and the linear city.

Living units are designed with large seamless windows that provide natural light to the living spaces, offer a wide-angled view over the Dungeness coastline, and serve as a screen. Double glazed units in-filled with special 3M angled film captures projected images onto the inner surface of the glass, transforming the window into a domestic entertainment unit. As the façade alternates between screen and window, living itself is described as a visual spectacle.

The Grand Walkway is a place of both material and intangible exchange, manifesting itself as a colon-

naded glazed atrium space. Units of consumption and exchange occupy either side of the walkway, with the outer walls clad with LCD screens in a continuous broadcast of news, announcements, music videos, performances, speeches, entertainment, financial market indexes and advertisements.

The temple is a transient space facilitating our constant need for communication, whereby one can wirelessly re-charge gadgets, work, contemplate, communicate, research, debate and exchange information. It is a prototypical agora of science and debate, of social exhibitionism and of technocratic worship.

Conclusion

Referencing Joseph Paxton's 'The Great Victorian Way', a utopian glazed covered walkway, the Linear City as link to satellite nuclear sites introduces a new typology of city expansion. It embraces the capital-driven market and technological interconnectivity that has appropriated a unique typology in our major cities. Our post industrialized economy forces us to intelligently adapt our existing conditions and waste production with our modern technology, in this case as a clean energy source capable of fuelling our current urbanization, demonstrating a resilience and adaptability in living and architecture.

ENDNOTES:

1 A total of 26 Magnox nuclear power reactors were constructed in the UK, which are housed by 11 power stations owned and operated by two nuclear site licensees of the NDA, namely BNFL and Magnox Electric plc.
"Magnox Electric plc's strategy for decommissioning its nuclear licensed sites", *Health and Safety Executive* (HSE), February 2002, pp.17
"Our Sites", accessed 17 October 2013, http://www.magnoxsites.co.uk/our-sites

2 "Magnox Electric plc's strategy for decommissioning its nuclear licensed sites", *Health and Safety Executive* (HSE), February 2002, pp.31-32

3 "Magnox Electric plc's strategy for decommissioning its nuclear licensed sites", *HSE,* February 2002

4 Energy figures from BNFL (British Nuclear Fuels Limited).

5 Calculation is based on average UK household energy consumption in 2010.

6 (Figures of waste and power production for Dungeness from BNFL.)

7 "New thermocell could harvest 'waste heat' ", accessed 11 August 2013, http://phys.org/news/2013-07-thermocell-harvest.html

8 "Ceramics: How They Work," *BBC4,* 3 September 2013

9 Ibid

FAST FORWARD FROM MACRO TO MICRO

NANOMATERIALS IN HERITAGE BUILDINGS

by SYLVIA LEYDECKER AND ANDREAS FRANKE

Historic monuments, old building structures and innovative nanomaterials harmonize well with one another. At first glance this may seem an unlikely combination, but on closer inspection it becomes clear that it offers promising potential:

Old buildings are not necessarily "old" in a negative sense, as in old and dilapidated. They are not blots on the landscape and they do not blight our cities. Likewise, their inhabitants do not see them as a troublesome burden. As a legacy of the past and a part of our cultural heritage they are highly prized and worth protecting. In most cases they have a distinctive charm, whether they are burgher's houses with ornamental stuccowork from the turn of the last century, colossal factory complexes from the industrial age, humble half-timbered buildings from medieval times or castles of the nobility. As historic monuments of their time, they are part of living history and as such are irreplaceable and valuable. While we have an obligation to conserve history, this does not have to be backwards-looking, a dogmatic preservation of tradition isolated from the here and now. Instead we need to integrate these buildings into the future. For a building to remain useful in the future, it must adapt – to the transformations of time and to the changes that new habits and ways of living bring with them. Adaptability

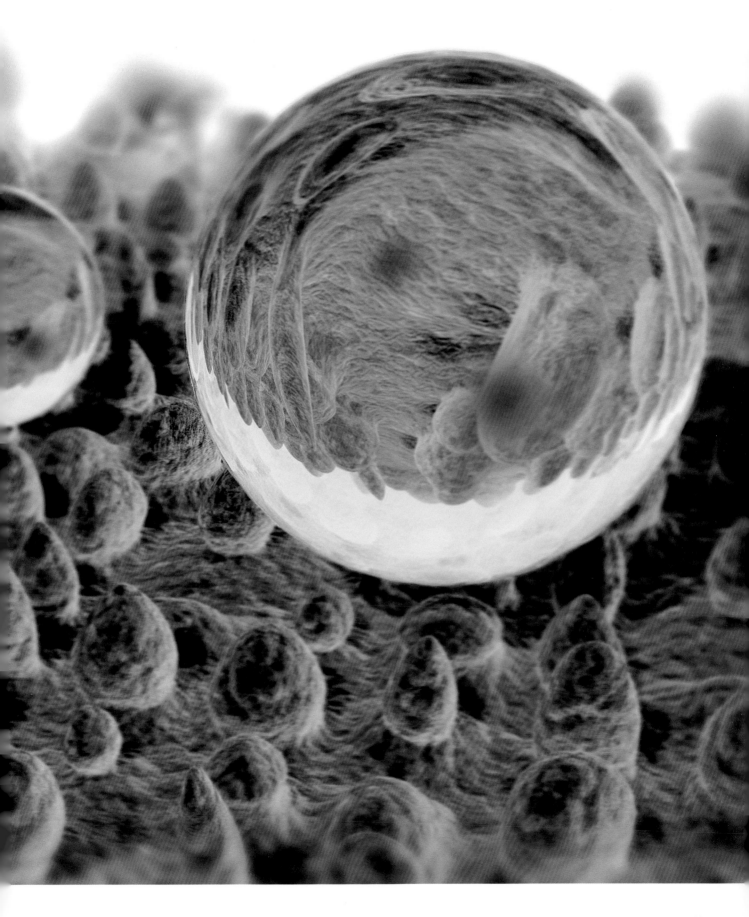

The Lotus effect

structures stand as well as delicate surface finishes and stucco elements or wall and ceiling murals, all of which must be documented and surveyed. The building's proportions are also a key characteristic as they are defined by the available building technology and the materials chosen for their construction. In the past, as today, the loadbearing capacity of a structure and the accompanying room spans were dictated by the technical possibilities of the day. All of these analyses are concerned with the coarse structure of the building, with its macrostructures. And this is the point – when the original substance of the building has been exposed and tells its story and when new building elements are about to be inserted – 'where it is appropriate' to consider new concepts and approaches to construction that combine traditional building methods and historic building materials with new constructions and innovative materials created as a product of high-tech processes: where we have the potential to achieve an inspired and entirely contemporary combination of macrostructures and microstructures. Today, as in the past, the use of forward-looking building technology not only has its purposes but can also contribute through a play of contrasts to the building's design. A space-age addition to a medieval ensemble, to use an exaggerated example, may at first seem a striking and perhaps discordant contrast but on closer inspection could be an ideal pair in which the innovations of each time are made legible. Today, as in the past and in the future, this is also our chance to use innovative materials and new developments to help buildings continue to exist sustainably in the future. Sustainability is not just about finding new uses for buildings to ensure their survival or about improving their energy performance; it is also about respecting the aesthetics of its function and associated characteristics such as the form and proportion of the building and the impression and proportions of the spaces it contains. This is where, through nanotechnology, microstructures offer possibilities for fulfilling all the above criteria and requirements and thus can be of use in historic buildings – for example in the form of vacuum insulation panels, aerogel-filled glazing panels, phase change materials and photo-catalytic self-cleansing surfaces. It is, of course, a balancing act: we don't want to eliminate the much-loved patina of the traces of the building's past and we still want to be able to see the age of a building at first glance. But surely we can still achieve more, and if so, of what? Of history or the space age? It would seem that there is as much a need to achieve a harmonious interaction between new and old and to adapt buildings to changing uses as there is a need to make intelligent use of energy without impacting on the specific character of the building. This will be essential for all buildings in future and that means that energy-efficient historic monuments that retain their unique character should no longer be an exception but the rule.

is the key to ensuring that a building continues to be filled with life and not merely that it survives over time as a museum. This means not just adapting to changing uses but also that we should be open to employing the useful properties of innovative building materials 'where they are appropriate'. What is particularly interesting in this context is the resulting symbiosis of tradition and innovation, of a historical legacy and forward-looking perspective.

The question is, of course, what does 'where appropriate' mean and where exactly does this apply? For this we need to get to the heart of the matter, both figuratively and literally, by looking at the actual building substance. In order to adequately work with and respect the essential qualities of a historical building, we first need to examine and reliably secure the original building substance. Very often, where buildings are converted, renovated, restored or revitalized, building works are first undertaken to remove building substance, for example from previous alterations. The remaining structures and building elements have endured the passage of time and retained their stability, and at the time of their construction must have represented the state of the art of construction and building technology. Measured surveys, damage appraisals and sometimes also archaeological investigations document the history and genesis of the entire building ensemble, of its parts and of the individual components that together make up the building. These investigations uncover hidden structures: rhythmic patterns of roof trusses made of steel or wood, foundations made of rough-hewn stone on which brickwork walls or irregular timber-frame

Continuing this chain of thought, the question arises as to how the preserved patina of the past and the new patina of today's innovative materials could look in future, and how they will look together. It would seem that the only true way would be to use the best technologies and products available in the respective time in order to most effectively ensure that existing buildings and historic monuments last into the future.

Amidst their newer contexts, historic monuments exude a charm and character that contrasts with their surroundings, creating a stimulating tension. The natural deterioration of a building in the past shows us which building elements are most durable and re-usable, and which of them are most able to be used in combination with new materials for the future – in terms of their function, construction, and also aesthetics. Something uniquely new arises in which technological microstructures in the form of innovative nanotechnology products offering a range of diverse functions exist in symbiosis with traditional static macrostructures. This opens up a range of ever-new and inspiring possibilities that

offer diverse, many-faceted and, above all, legible ways of combining the macro and micro in a building and that can be individually applied at different scales, whether for historic building ensembles or complex, historical urban constellations. Nevertheless, there are certainly situations in both macro and microstructures in which traditional approaches are more appropriate than innovation, and where reconstruction is the more appropriate path.

The use of nanotechnological materials on their own is just the beginning of this new technological revolution; the use of nanomaterials in existing buildings and historic monuments represents a much more diverse and multi-layered revolution in the way we design buildings. The development of new materials and functional surface coatings will in future have a considerable impact on working with existing buildings, and especially in the realm of the conversion and renovation of historic buildings. The way in which we build and what we build will be influenced significantly. In order to achieve forward-looking and pioneering work in the realm of existing buildings, interior designers

Modern housing will be the future's heritage, Hong Kong

reason for employing nanomaterials is their contribution to energy-efficiency. Other promising reasons are the reduced consumption of resources and better sustainability, not to mention the reduced cost of the ongoing maintenance of buildings (a primary motivator). In the construction sector, innovations are slow to be adopted in practice, and when they are, then typically for new buildings. Existing buildings are not generally the focus of innovations, and historic monuments even less so. But it is in precisely this area that there will be greater demand in future: in technological terms these buildings are falling behind and becoming less and less attractive – however charming they may be – for investors, owners and building operators. The future, however, has a solution for this dilemma that is already available today: while their full potential for architecture in general has yet to be fully explored, in the context of the macrostructures of historic buildings, for example solid, structurally-sound oak beam constructions or rough-hewn stone masonry, the use of dynamic materials whose properties can alter in response to changes in temperature or (air) humidity is potentially game-changing. It represents a significant change in how we perceive and will experience the

legibility of time in historic buildings. The atmosphere of a space as a whole as well as how we experience the parts of an interior will be most special, an encounter of the third kind. A spatial and aesthetic interaction between the ages, the past and the present, as well as between the user and the 'smart material' which, as a product of developments in nanotechnology, possesses extremely fine microstructures that have a protective or insulating capacity. These are just some examples of aspects that not only warrant the coexistence and combination of micro and macrostructures but also stand to enrich the fields of architecture and interior design as a whole and, in the spirit of the historic monument, will keep them alive in more senses than one.

In this context, nanomaterials offer a broad range of functions that, when applied appropriately, have distinct advantages. The currently available spectrum of functions ranges from those that are comparatively well known, such as self-cleaning surfaces, to innovative niche products such as building elements made of carbon. Of all the nanomaterial-based functions that are now available on the market, the most well established is the aforementioned self-cleaning surface treatment, which is now employed around the world. With the help of this invisible layer, it is possible to reduce or even avoid all kinds of dirt and soiling. Hydrophobic, water-repellent surface coatings that employ the so-called Lotus Effect are becoming ever more popular. Although this term is actually a trademark, and thus only actually present in selected products, the name is so memorable that it has become emblematic for nanotechnology as a whole. Natural Lotus

and architects will need to expand their horizons and rethink how they approach the subject of historic building conservation. Without embracing technological advancements there will be no progress. And that has always been the case: for as long as we have been building, we have developed ever more advanced building methods, constructions and materials – from locally-available and natural-occurring materials such as stone, wood or plant fibers to high-tech and smart materials. Materials based on nanotechnology are the product of one of the key technologies of the 21st century and as such definitively part of the future. As with all new technologies, the benefits and dangers need to be weighed up because the opportunities it presents are too attractive to be ignored. The primary

flower surfaces are micro-rough and their self-cleaning property is a product of their hydrophobicity. Artificial Lotus Effect surfaces function the same way, but are unfortunately susceptible to mechanical abrasion and unlike their cousin in the natural world are not able to heal themselves. Lotus Effect surfaces are often confused with so-called easy-to-clean surfaces that have a reduced surface attraction and, like the Lotus Effect, are hydrophobic, causing water to run off in droplets. Lotus Effect pain ts have been available on the market for more than ten years but are still regarded as innovative and are ideal for use on the façades of

historic buildings were water tends to accumulate, such as on the surface of horizontal cornices. In the context of historic monument preservation the use of such paint avoids the need for a sheet metal zinc cornice covering with rainwater drip, which falsifies the original appearance of the building and is not authentic to the original structure. Photocatalytic (semi) self-cleaning surfaces employ a different technique and are able to reduce dirt accumulation by decomposing organic dirt and allowing the loose dirt particles to wash off from its hydrophilic surface on a film of water the next time the surface is wetted. Although none of these surfaces are completely

Restored half-timbered house of 1728 and its extension, Kreuzau, Germany

self-cleansing, the cleaning interval can be extended significantly: a coat of façade paint, for example, lasts much longer and needs to be repainted less often. Similarly, glazing remains cleaner for longer, as do roof tiles. Self-cleaning surfaces are therefore an elegant solution for maintaining the well cared-for appearance of historic buildings. Surfaces that are prone to algae formation can also be given an additional anti-bacteria treatment.

With respect to energy-efficiency, historic monuments and many normal existing buildings are generally inadequately insulated. Where buildings are of historical architectural value, one cannot simply follow the general trend of applying thermal matting as insulation to the façades. This approach is not appropriate as it obscures the face of the building and its appearance in the urban context, in short robbing it of its cultural identity. Another approach is to dispense with

external insulation completely and to apply insulation on the interior that does not impact on the outer façade. High-performance insulation materials such as vacuum insulation panels (VIPs) are a new option that provides good insulation at very thin thicknesses. Almost ten times thinner than conventional thermal insulation, they take up much less space, leaving more of the interior available as usable and therefore lettable space, which is especially important in cities. Glazing that contains aerogel offers much improved insulation while allowing a soft diffuse light to illuminate the room. Phase Change Materials (PCMs) change their aggregate state from fluid to solid and back and are bound in microcapsules, allowing them to serve as a temperature buffer absorbing heat, as well as vice versa, giving off heat: as such they can be used for both heating and cooling. PCM additives can be found in

Steel footbridge in a historic barn 1778, Düren, Germany

plasters, building boards and foamed concrete blocks, all building materials that are already commonly used in the renovation of old buildings. Thermochromic glass reduces the effect of the sun, avoiding the need for blinds, curtains and other added elements. In the field of conservation, thermochromic glass can be used to protect room where direct sunlight can be damaging. Electrochromic glass can also be darkened on demand, and does not require electricity to retain its state. It likewise avoids the need for blinds, but it still requires an intervention in the building substance during installation. Anti-fingerprint surfaces can be applied to glass or stainless steel and significantly reduce the visibility of fingerprints. Many historic buildings are repeatedly sprayed with graffiti and are constantly being cleaned. Conventional protective coatings function as a sacrificial layer that needs to be removed. A disadvantage is that they are not vapor permeable, preventing the building from giving off moisture as it should. Nanomaterial-based anti-graffiti coatings on the other hand provide the necessary protection and are simultaneously vapor-permeable, preserving the characteristics of the building substance. Hydrophobic coatings for historic buildings frontages made of brick or wood are a further way of improving the durability of exposed building elements. Other interesting applications using conductive coatings and lighting will become available in the future. Currently, effect-pigments and dichroitic surfaces can be used to dynamically change the appearance of surfaces. Super lightweight and strong materials such as Ultra-High-Performance-Concrete (UHPC) and carbon building elements offer potential for building very slender new constructions, which have potential for use in the extensions to existing buildings. In addition to the aforementioned functions, a range of further innovations are expected to be make their way from the realm of the science community to industry and the market place, fuelled by enlightened designers, architects and clients. The undertaking of applied research and the transferal of findings into market-ready products are therefore beneficial from both a constructional and aesthetic perspective.

Buildings that have stood the test of time and are today regarded as historic monuments were typically state-of-the-art examples of the outstanding technology of their day. By the same means, the modern-day renovation and conversion of historic buildings should ideally adhere to the same principle, employing the most innovative construction methods in the interest of preserving such monuments for the future. Then as now, the building construction and its later renovation are innovative examples of the best of what is possible at the respective time. Sooner or later both will be recede into the past – it is just a matter of time until the apparent contradictions have merged into a harmonious whole.

Laser cut steel stair in a half timbered house 1728, Kreuzau, Germany

TRANSCENDING TIME
CAN RIBAS, PALMA DE MALLORCA

by MARKUS BERGER

PHOTO ESSAY
Can Ribas, Public space and industrial heritage

LOCATION
La Soledat, Palma de Mallorca, Spain

CURRENT USE
public space, (social housing, civic centre in phase 2)

PRIOR USE
Can Ribas textile factory, built in 1851 for the production of wool blankets

CONVERSION DATE
2011

ARCHITECTURE FIRM
Jaime J. Ferrer Forés

PHOTOS
José Hevia

With the dual objective of industrial heritage preservation and neighborhood revitalization, Can Ribas is a project of design and social resilience. A former textile factory built in 1951 for the production of woolen blankets, the site was abandoned in the 70's and acquired by Patronat Municipal de l'Habitatge, a local municipal housing trust, with the goal to develop social housing units. The project, won in a 2005 competition by Jamie J. Ferrer Fores architect, is delineated in two stages; the urban public spaces and industrial heritage site were completed in 2011 and the social housing and civic center will be part of a later phase.

In the first phase, Industrial Heritage Preservation is achieved through thoughtful and bold design interventions that transform a former industrial complex into a new urban corridor and public space. Utilizing traces of the industrial complex, the urban plan opens and reconnects the former industrial site with the Le Soledat neighborhood through the creation of a passage between Brotad Street and the recreational and cultural facilities of the area. The proposed elements of the second phase will further act as a revitalization agent within the decayed neighborhood.

The approach of Can Ribas demonstrates the ability of lost and abandoned structures that once separated communities to re-engage, re-vitalize, and re-connect people and its history.

PROJECT CREDITS, INFORMATION
AND BIBLIOGRAPHIES

EDITORIAL

illustrations by_ Roberto Collovà
see project credits: "Taking on the shape of things" on page 140

WIDE OPEN

illlustrations by_ Marco Vanucci | website_ www.opensystems-a.com

THE URBAN BACKDOOR

Illustrations by_ Fabrizio Gesuelli and Chiara Andreotti (p. 14) | image source_ Last Judgment at the Sistine Chapel by Michelangelo, Wikimedia commons; The Last Judgment at the Arena Chapel (Cappella Scrovegni), in Padua by Giotto, Wikimedia Commons | Parkour vault by Alexandre Ferreira/http://www.flickr.com/photos/amf/146161759/ cc-by-2.0

BIBLIOGRAPHY:

-Augé, Marc. Non-Places. Second English language edition. ed. London ; New York: Verso, 2008.
-Blech, Benjamin, and Roy Doliner. The Sistine Secrets : Michelangelo's Forbidden Messages in the Heart of the Vatican / Benjamin Blech & Roy Doliner. New York : HarperOne, c2008.1st ed., 2008. BibliographiesNon-fiction.
-Blume, Andrew Charles. The Sistine Chapel, Dynastic Ambition, and the Cultural Patronage of Sixtus IV. 2007. Book.
-Brown, Steven D. "Michel Serres : Science, Translation and the Logic of the Parasite (English)." -Michel Serres : science, traduction et logique du parasite (French) 19, no. 3 (01/2002 2002): 1-27.
-De Landa, Manuel. Philosophy and Simulation : The Emergence of Synthetic Reason. London: Continuum, 2011. Book.
-De Landa, Manuel. "Beyond the Problematic of Legitimacy: Military Influences on Civilian Society." 117-28: Duke University Press, 2005.
-De Maio, Romeo. Michelangelo E La Controriforma / Romeo De Maio; Con 48 Tavole Fuori Testo. Collezione Storica. Roma ; Bari : Laterza, 1978., 1978. Book.
-Deleuze, Gilles. The Fold : Leibniz and the Baroque / Gilles Deleuze ; Foreword and Translation by Tom Conley. London : Athlone, 1993., 1993. BibliographiesNon-fiction.
-Deleuze, Gilles, and Félix Guattari. A Thousand Plateaus : Capitalism and Schizophrenia / Gilles Deleuze, Félix Guattari; Translation and Foreword by Brian Massumi. London : Athlone Press, 1988., 1988. Book.
-Mancinelli, F., G. Colalucci, and N. Gabrielli. Last Judgement. Giunti, 1994.
-Michelangelo - the Sistine Chapel : The Restoration of the Ceiling Frescoes. 1. Report on the Restauration. Pontifical Monuments, Museums and Galleries. Canova, 2001. Book.
-Munari, Bruno. Fantasia / Bruno Munari. Universale Laterza: 385. Roma ; Bari : Laterza, 1977. 1. ed., 1977. Non-fiction.
-Nibby, A. Analisi Storico-Topografico-Antiquaria Della Carta De'dintorni Di Roma. Roma: Tipografia delle Belle Arti,1837.
-Radford, Gary P., and Marie L. Radford."Structuralism,Post-Structuralism,and the Library: De Saussure and Foucault (English)."Journal of documentation 61,no.1(01/20052005): 60-78.
-"Review: Noam Chomsky, Three Models for the Description of Language." Association for Symbolic Logic 1958-03, 1958.
-Saussure, Ferdinand de, Haun Saussy, Perry Meisel, and Wade Baskin. Course in General Linguistics. New York: Columbia University Press, 2011. Book.
-Serres, Michel, and Lawrence R. Schehr. The Parasite / Michel Serres ; Translated, with Notes, by Lawrence R. Schehr. Baltimore ; London : Johns Hopkins University Press, [1982], ©1982., 1982. Non-fiction.
-Tschumi, Bernard. Architecture and Disjunction / Bernard Tschumi. Cambridge, Mass. : MIT Press, 1996.

CORAL TYPOLOGY

computer generated images by_ Richard Goodwin pty ltd

BIBLIOGRAPHY:

-Till J. Architecture Depends, Cambridge, Massachusetts: The MIT Press, 2009.
-Delleuze G. & Guttari F. A Thousand Plateaus: Capitalism and Schizophrenia, Minneapolis: University of Minnesota Press, 1987.
-Foster H. Prosthetic Gods, Cambridge, Massachusetts: The MIT Press, 2004.
-Wigley M. Constant's New Babylon, The Hyper-Architecture of Desire, Rotterdam: Witte de With, Centre for contemporary art / oio Publishers 1998.
-Zizek S. Violence, six sideways reflections, London, Profile Books Ltd 2009;
-Goodwin R. Porosity: The Architecture of Invagination, Melbourne: RMIT University Press 2011.

JAPAN'S ARCHITECTURAL GENOME

image source_ aerial view: (p. 27) http://commons.wikimedia.org/wiki/File: Ise_Shrine_Naiku_1953-.-8-.-26.jpg, accessed 12.09.2013 (copyright: public domain);
pagoda drawing (p. 30): http://en.wikipedia.org/wiki/File:Horyu-.-ji06s3200.jpg, accessed 04.03.2014, (dated: 21.10.2006, author: 663highland, copyright: GNU Free Documentation License);
"Tokyo Bay Project" (p.28): Kawasumi Kobayashi Kenji Photograph Office Co. (author: Akio Kawasuma);
Tokyo Sky Tree (p. 31): http://upload.wikimedia.org/wikipedia/commons/b/b2/Tokyo_Sky_Tree_2012_%E2%85%A 2.JPG, accessed 08.09.2013 (copyright: Creative Commons Attribution-. Share Alike 3.0 Unported license)
Pagoda of Horyu-ji (p. 29): GFDL+creative commons2.5, Wikimedia Commons

BIBLIOGRAPHY:

-Arata Isozaki, Japan-ness in Architecture (Cambridge, London: MIT Press, 2006)
-Hidenobu Jinnai, Tokyo, A Spatial Anthropology (Berkeley, Los Angeles, London: University of California Press, 1995)
-Rem Koolhaas, Hans Ulrich Obrist, Project Japan. Metabolism Talks... (Köln:Taschen, 2011)

-Nipponia No. 33, June 15, 2005, accessed 08.09.2013, http://web-japan.org/nipponia/nipponia33/en/topic/index.html#fig1
-Fujita K., Hanazato T., Sakamoto I., "Earthquake response monitoring and seismic performance of five-storied timber pagoda", 13th World Conference on Earthquake Engineering Vancouver, B.C., Canada August 1-6, 2004, Paper No. 54.
-Masako Minami (Senior Structural Engineer, Arup Japan), "Mode Gakuen Cocoon Tower – An Iconic -High-rise Campus in a Dense City", *Steel Construction Today & Tomorrow*, No. 25, Tokyo, December 2008, 11-14
-Katsuhiko Yamawaki, Toru Kobori (Structural Engineering Dpt., Nikken Sekkei Ltd.), "Mode Gakuen Spiral Towers – An Approach to Structural Design for Realizing Advanced Structural Configurations in Earthquake-prone Countries", *Steel Construction Today & Tomorrow*, No. 25, Tokyo, December 2008, 5-10
-Nikken Sekkei, "Structural Technology", accessed 08.09.2013, http://www.nikken.co.jp/ensk/skytree/structure/

IN BETWEEN

name of photographer_ Scott Kalner (p. 36, 38r); author (p. 38l) | image source_ 2400 Block of Jefferson St., Philadelphia (p. 32) housing association of Delaware Valley [copyright: Temple University Libraries] | illustrations by_ author

FOSTERING RESILIENCE IN A VULNERABLE TERRAIN

location_ Paris, France | name of photographer_ Pari Rahi

PRESERVING THE FLOW

location_ Mississsippi delta Louisiana | illustration by_ (p. 48): ParadoXcity studio 2011 Mississippi, Student: M. Geffel; (p. 50) ParadoXcity studio 2011 Mississippi, Student: R. Dye; (p. 49) author; ParadoXcity_ (p.51) studio 2011 Mississippi, Student: D. Lebedeva & D. Deavitt; (p. 46) Harold Fisk for the Mississippi River Commission, 1943, Baton Rouge; (p.49) by author.

BIBLIOGRAPHY:

-Morton, Timothy (2013) *HyperObjects: Philosophy and Ecology after the End of the World*. University of Minnesota Press.
-Michel Serres (1995) *The Natural Contract*. (translated by E. MacArthur and W. Paulson) University of Michigan Press.
-Latour, Bruno (1993) *We Have Never Been Modern*. Hemel Hempstead: Harvester Wheatsheaf.
-Jonas, Wolfgang and Grand, Simon (Ed.) (2012) *Mapping Design Research* Birkhaeuser, 2012.
-EPA (1987) *Saving Louisiana's Coastal Wetlands*. The Need for a Long-Term Plan of Action.
-Naveh, Liebermann (1984) *Landscape Ecology,* Springer New York p. 59-63.
-Waddington, C. H. (1974) "A Catastrophe Theory of Evolution". *Annals of the New York Academy of Sciences* 231: 32-42.

REMAPPING THE MIDLANDS

location_ The Midlands of Ireland | photos by_ AP+E | illustrations by_ AP+E | other collaborators_ Miriam Delaney | website address of design firm_ www.APplusE.eu | funding by_ The Royal Institute of Architects of Ireland (RIAI), the Irish Government Policy on Architecture and the Housing and Sustainable Communities Agency, Ireland

LESSONS FROM QUEENSLAND FOR VIABLE FUTURES

location_ Queensland, Australia | name of photographer_ Tony Fry (p. 61-65) Naomi Hay (p. 67) | website_ www.design-futures.com.au (Design Futures Program, Queensland College of Art, Griffith University)

RESILIENCE:

name of photographer_ Frank Thiel

BIBLIOGRAPHY:

-Bhamra, R., S. Dani and K. Burnard, "Resilience: the concept, a literature review and future directions." *International Journal of Production Research* 49, 19 (2011): 5375-5394.
-Buizer, M., B. Arts, and K. Kok. "Governance, scale, and the environment: the importance of recognizing knowledge claims in transdisciplinary arenas." *Ecology and Society* 16 (2011). http://www.ecologyandsociety.org/vol16/iss1/art21/.
-Deprés, Carole, Geneviève Vachon and Andrée Fortin. 2011. "Implementing Transdisciplinarity: Architecture and Urban Planning at Work." In Isabelle Doucet and Nel Janssens, eds. *Transdisciplinary knowledge production in architecture and urbanism, Towards hybrid modes of inquiry*. 33-49.
-Folke, C. "Resilience: the emergence of a perspective for social-ecological systems analysis." *Global Environmental Change* 16 (2006): 253-267.
-. "How resilient are ecosystems to global environmental change?" *Sustainability Science* 5 (2010): 151–154.
-, and L. Gunderson. "Facing global change through social-ecological research." *Ecology and Society* 11, 2 (2006). http://www.ecologyandsociety.org/vol11/iss2/art43/.
-, S. Carpenter, B. Walker, M. Scheffer, T. Chapin, and J. Rockstrom. "Resilience thinking: integrating resilience, adaptability and transformability." *Ecology and Society* 15, 4 (2010) http://www.ecologyandsociety.org/vol15/iss4/art20/.
-Fry, T. "Getting over architecture: Thinking, surmounting and redirecting." In *Transdisciplinary knowledge production in architecture and urbanism: Towards hybrid modes of inquiry*, edited by Isabelle Doucet and Nel Janssens, 16-32. New York: Springer, 2011.
-Gunderson, L. H., and C. S. Holling, editors. *Panarchy: understanding transformations in human and natural systems*. Washington D.C.: Island Press, 2002.
-Holling, C.S., L.H. Gunderson, D. Ludwig. "In Search of a Theory of Adaptive Change." In *Panarchy: Understanding Transformations in Human and Natural Systems*, edited by C.S. Holling, L.H. Gunderson, D. Ludwig, 3-24. Washington D.C.: Island Press, 2002.
-Hommels, A. "Studying obduracy in the city: Toward a productive fusion between technology studies and urban studies." *Science, Technology & Human Values*. 30 (2005): 323-351.
-Hughes, T.P., Carpenter, S., Rockström, S., Scheffer, M., Walker, B. 2013. "Multiscale regime shifts and planetary boundaries." *Trends in Ecology & Evolution* 28, 7 (2013): 389-395.
-Kohler, N. and U. Hassler. "The building stock as a research object' in *Building Research & Information* 30, 4 (2002): 226–236.
-Lorch, R. "A research strategy for the built environment?" ARQ 7, 2 (2003): 119-125.
-Lowe, R. "Preparing the built environment for climate change." Building Research & Information 31, 4-5 (2003): 195–199.
-Martin-Breen, P., and J.M. Anderies. "Resilience: A Literature Review." *Rockefeller Foundation* (2011) http://www.rockefellerfoundation.org/news/publications/resilience-literature-review.
-McDonough, W. and M. Braungart. "Eco Effectiveness: A New Design Strategy." In *Sustainable Architecture White Papers,* edited by D. Brown, M. Fox and M.R. Pelletier, 1-4. NY: Earth Pledge, 2005.
-McShane, C. *Down the asphalt path: The automobile and the American city.* New York, Columbia University Press, 1994.
-Moffatt, S., and Kohler, N. "Conceptualizing the built envi-

ronment as a social ecological system." *Building Research & Information* 36, 3 (2008): 248-268.

-Olson, P., L. Gunderson, S. Carpenter, P. Ryan, L. Lebel, C. Folke and C. Holling. "Shooting the Rapids: Navigating Transitions to Adaptive Governance of Social-ecological Systems." *Ecology and Society*. 11, 1 (2006). http://www.ecologyandsociety.org/vol11/iss1/art18/.

-Peeples, M. A., C. M. Barton, and S. Schmich. "Resilience lost: intersecting land use and landscape dynamics in the prehistoric southwestern United States." *Ecology and Society* 11, 2 (2006). http://www.ecologyandsociety.org/vol11/iss2/art22/.

-Pendlebury, J. *Conservation in the Age of Consensus*. Abingdon: Routledge, 2009.

-Rintala, S. "Edge on paracentric architecture." *Topos* 70 (2010): 48-55.

-Sachs, W. "Sustainable Development and the Crisis of Nature: On the Political Anatomy of an Oxymoron." In *Living with Nature Environmental Politics as Cultural Discourse*, edited by F. Fischer and M. Hajer, 23-41. Oxford: Oxford UP, 1999.

-Smith, A., and A. Stirling. "The politics of social-ecological resilience and sustainable socio-technical transitions." *Ecology and Society* 15, 1 (2010). http://www.ecologyandsociety.org/vol15/iss1/art11/.

-Voß, J.P. "Shaping socio-ecological transformation: The case for innovating governance." Paper presented at the Open Science Meeting of the International Human Dimensions Program of Global Environmental Change Research, Montreal, Canada, October 18, 2003.

-Walker, B., C. S. Holling, S.R. Carpenter, and A.Kinzig. "Resilience, Adaptation and Transformability in Social-ecological Systems." *Ecology and Society* 9, 2 (2004). http://www.ecologyandsociety.org/vol9/iss2/art5.

-Walker, B., L. Gunderson, A. Kinzig, C. Folke, S. Carpenter, and L. Schultz. "A Handful of Heuristics and Some Propositions for Understanding Resilience in Social-Ecological Systems." *Ecology and Society* 11, 1 (2006). http://www.ecologyandsociety.org/vol11/iss1/art13/.

THE NEW PROJECTS

name of project_ St. Cloud Apt. and Thai Xuan Village | location_ Huston TX | illustrations by_ Rose Lee (p. 78), Susan Rogers (p. 81) | name of photographer_ Hana Abuelaish (p. 80)

EXILED

location_ New York, NY | name of photographer_ Gregory Marinic

TAKING ON THE SHAPE OF THINGS

Pages 88, 98-101
Reconstruction of the Mother Church 1984-98 | location_ Salemi (TP), Sicilia | client_ Ordinariato Diocesano di Mazara del Vallo (TP) | architects_ Álvaro Siza Vieira, Roberto Collovà, with U.T.Curia Mazara del Vallo | construction administration_ 1°/2° lotto, Roberto Collovà / U.T.Curia Mazara del Vallo - 3° lotto, Roberto Collovà | team_ O.Marrone, V.Trapani, E.Tocco, G.Ruggieri, F.Tramonte, G.Malventano, M.Ciaccio, A.Lo Sardo, K.Muscarella, R.Viviano. | contractor_ geom. Melchiorre Armata, Salemi | lighting_ Álvaro Siza Vieira, Roberto Collovà (design), O-Luce Milano (produzione) | name of photographer_ Roberto Collovà

Pages 90, 91, 97
Recovery and reconstruction of the buildings of Case Di Stefano 1982-97| location_ Gibellina (TP), Sicilia | client_ Comune di Gibellina| architects_ Roberto Collovà, Marcella Aprile, Teresa La Rocca construction administration_ Roberto Collovà, Marcella Aprile, Teresa La Rocca | design team_ V.Acierno, M.Ciaccio, A.D'Amico, L.Felli, M.Gurrieri, M.Leonardi, S.Marina, F.Nicita, L.Raspanti, E.Tocco, A.Lo Sardo, R.Viviano | name of photographer_ Roberto Collovà

Pages 92-95
Urban systems in the Historic Center of Gela 1993-12 | location_ Gela (CL), Sicilia client: Comune di Gela architect and construction administration_ Roberto Collovà design team_ G.Fascella, L.Foto, A.Molica Bisci, R.De Simone, M.Di Gregorio, M.Enia, S.Perrotta, S.Urbano lighting_ Roberto Collovà (design), O-Luce Milano (produzione) name of photographer_ Roberto Collovà

Pages 96, 97, 104, 105
Belice '80, Exhibit at the Museo Civico "Ludovico Corrao" di Gibellina | name of photographer_ Roberto Collovà

Pages 102, 103
The Urban Park of Salemi, Garden of the Carmine   (1° intervention):Outdoor Theater 1981/1986 | location_ Salemi (TP), Sicilia | client_ Comune di Salemi | architects_ Roberto Collovà, Marcella Aprile, Francesco Venezia | construction administration_ Roberto Collovà, Marcella Aprile | design team_ Anna Alì, Oreste Marrone | name of photographer_ Roberto Collovà

BEIT BEIRUT

name of project_ Beit Beirut, previously known as Beit Barakat | location_ Beirut, Lebanon | name of design firm_ Youssef Haidar Architects | name of key architects/designers involved in project_ Mona Hallak ; activist_ Youssef Aftimos | name of original architects_ Fouad Kozah | name of owner_ Beirut Municipality | photo and illustrations by_ courtesy of architect | year completed_ 2015 | cost of construction_ $20 million | website address of design firm_ www.youssef-haidar.com

TYPOLOGY IN CRISIS

name of project_ cooling tower in Beringen | location_ Beringen, Belgium |name of photographer_ Lore Mellemans (coverphoto), Isabelle Van Assche (p. 113, 114), Heekyung Kim (p.116) | article collaboration_ Koenraad Van Cleempoel

LIVING FUEL

name of project_ the interim linear city | location_ London GB | illustrations by_ Emily Yeung | website address of design firm_ http://emilyeung.wordpress.com.

FAST FORWARD FROM MACRO TO MICRO

name of photographer_ Andreas Franke (P. 127-129, Sylvia Leydecker (P. 124-126) | image source_ William Thielicke (p. 123), Wikimedia Commonns

TRANSCENDING TIME

name of project_ Can Ribas | location_ La Soledat, Palma de Mallorca, Spain | current use_ public space and industrial heritage; (social housing, civic center in phase 2) | prior use_ can ribas textile factory (built in 1851 for the production of wool blankets) | conversion date_ 2011 | architecture firm_ jaime J. Ferrer Forés | collaborators_ Toni Vilanova (industrial heritage consultant); Yolanda Ortega Sanz (architect); Maria Antonia Palmer Porcell and Bartomeu Bonet Palmer (quantity surveyors); Antoni Ramis Arrom and Esteban Pisano Porada (services) | photographer_ José Hevia

COLOPHON

AUTHORS

Chiara Andreotti holds a Master's degree with distinction in Architecture from the Faculty of Architecture of Rome "La Sapienza". She also holds a diploma with distinction in Architectural Heritage and Landscape from the Postgraduate School in Architectural Heritage and Landscape, University of Rome "La Sapienza". Her interests are prevalently focussed on restoration, conservation and digital surveying with 3d laser scanner. Over the last year she has been working on reconstruction plans for several towns in Abruzzo, Italy, hit by an earthquake in 2009. Her thesis resulted in awards in two different competitions in 2010 and her research regarding both restoration of historical buildings and techniques for 3d digital surveying are published.

Krishna Bharathi is an American artist and architect who draws on experience gained from working as both a lead designer and field architect in multiple building typologies and planning scales in the U.S., Europe, and Asia. Krishna has a Bachelor of Psychology from the University of Chicago and a Master of Architecture from the University of Washington. Currently she is a doctoral research fellow supported by NTNU's Centre for Technology and Society, as well as, the Norwegian Research Centre on Zero Emission Buildings. In 2012 she was an invited exchange researcher to the Swiss Federal Institute of Technology (ETH Zürich) under the EU Erasmus Program. Currently, she is a visiting scholar to Columbia University under the endorsement of Kenneth Frampton. She lives in Zürich.

Jeffrey Bolhuis and Laurence Lord founded the studio Architecture Practice + Experimentation, a design and research studio based in Amsterdam and Copenhagen, working across the boundaries of architecture, urban design and regional redevelopment. The studio's agenda is to pursue architecture that stimulates new forms of community and social interaction concerned with provoking use, involvement and appropriation. Architecture Practice + Experimentation creates spaces, buildings and frameworks that are open to multiple interpretations and the dialogue between a diverse range of inhabitants in contemporary society.

Roberto Collovà is an Italian architect whose expansive body of work includes urban design, landscape design, furniture and photography. He is the author of *Piccole figure che passano*. He also writes for different journals in Italy and elsewhere. He has taught at the Facoltà di Architettura di Palermo and at the Academia di Architettura of Mendrisio in Switzerland as well as in institutions that include Barcelona, Lisbon, Las Palmas, Venice. His work was exhibited at the Venice Biennale and the Milan Triennale. His many awards include the Premio IN_ARCH for Design, the Premio Gubbio for architecture in historic centers, finalists in the Mies van der Rohe Award in 1990, finalist in the Italian Architectural Gold Medal Award 2003, winner of the Competition internazionale Diagonal, Barcellona 1989, winner of the Competition *Una via, tre piazze*, Gela 1993, winner of the Competition for the Masterplan at S. Cesarea Terme 2007. He was on the jury for the Mies van der Rohe Award 2005, BSI Swiss Architectural Award 2008 and for the Young Architects Program MAXXI / MoMa Ps 2011-2013.

Miriam Delaney, MA, BArch, MRIAI is a lecture and studio tutor in Dublin School of Architecture, having previously taught in University College Dublin and Queens University Belfast. She has co-authored *Studio Craft and Technique* and is currently conducting research into architectural representation.

Andreas Franke studied at University of Applied Sciences/ Trier, Düsseldorf and Detmold, Germany. His work is focused on comprehensive architectural and interior design concepts, adaptive reuse and historic preservation in combination with contemporary additions. Andreas Franke is active member of BDIA (German Association of Interior Architects). Various projects and professional contributions were published in relevant architectural and interior design magazines/ books.

Tony Fry BA (Hons). MA., PhD., is a designer, cultural theorist and educator. He leads the 'Design Futures' program at Queensland College of Art and directed the Griffith University, AusAID funded research and development project to create an academy of creative industries in East Timor. He continues the work with the project as an adviser to the Timorese government. Tony was the founding director of the EcoDesign Foundation, Sydney (1991-2001) and formerly Adjunct Professor, Faculty of Design, Architecture and Building, University of Technology, Sydney, (1998-2001); Honorary Research Associate, University of Sydney (1996-2001); Associate Director. University of Sydney National Key Centre of Design Quality (1991-92); Senior Lecturer in Design History and Theory, Power Institute, University of Sydney (1985-96). He has held visiting professorships and fellowships at universities in Asia, Europe and the USA. Tony is the author of ten books and numerous other publications.

Fabrizio Gesuelli holds a Master's degree in Architecture and a BS in Interior Design from the Faculty of

Architecture of Rome, University of Rome "La Sapienza". He is currently a PhD student in Architecture at the University of Edinburgh. As PhD candidate, his research involves the study of protest and how the latter tends to generate mechanisms of transformation. In particular, focusing on the role of medium, his research investigates the public space as mediating term between users and architectural object and how the replacement of this mediating figure can be transposed into architectural design. He is author of an article published in the *International Journal of Computer Information Technology*, regarding the use of new technologies in architectural design.

Richard Goodwin has over 30 years of practice as an internationally exhibiting artist and architect, Goodwin has sustained a prolific and award winning practice provoking boundaries between art and architecture. In 1996 Goodwin established the Porosity Studio at the College of Fine Arts within the University of New South Wales where he currently holds the position of Professor of Fine Arts and Design. He teaches part-time via intensive, international and multi-disciplinary studios providing a unique context for the renegotiation of delineations between art, architecture and urbanism.

Dana Hamdan is a recent graduate from the Interior Architecture department at Rhode Island School of Design, Providence, RI. After receiving her Bachelor of Architecture from the American University of Beirut, Lebanon, she worked for two years at a local multi-disciplinary engineering firm, SETSintl. She was a member of the architecture and planning department where she had the chance to work on diverse architectural and renovation projects. As an emerging architect her fondness for adaptive reuse has grown into a desire to be much more heavily involved in the field. It is a strategy that responds to today's world's economic and sustainability concerns. She came to value the neglected architectural heritage of her home country, Lebanon, that is being demolished. In August 2013 Dana joined Gensler, a world renowned architecture firm, where she hopes to learn more about adaptive reuse, and looks to research through design about ways to preserve and reuse the built heritage. She plans to return to Lebanon in the future and be involved in academia, and try to reinstate the mentality of preservation in the architectural education.

Sally Harrison is Associate Professor of Architecture in the Tyler School of Art, Temple University, and a Registered Architect. She has professional and teaching expertise in social impact design, sustainable urban design, and urban history/theory. She is the director and co-founder of The Urban Workshop, an interdisciplinary university-based practice that undertakes collaborative, community-centered research and design in underserved postindustrial neighborhoods. Her design and scholarship is published in numerous books and journals and has been recognized in national, international and regional design awards programs.

Naomi Hay is a lecturer in Interior Environments within the Design Futures program at Queensland College of Art, Griffith University. Naomi has a Bachelor Degree in the Built Environment and a Master of Design Futures (Hons) and has worked as a practicing interior designer across a broad spectrum of projects throughout Australia and Asia. She is enrolled as a PhD candidate at Griffith University with a research focus in the role of design in pre-emptive disaster strategy and strengthening resilience of vulnerable communities towards sustainable futures.

Sylvia Leydecker studied at University of Applied Sciences/Wiesbaden, Germany and University Trisakti/Jakarta/Indonesia before setting up her studio 100% interior in Cologne. She is working on corporate interiors, focussed on healthcare and regarded as leading for hospitals in Germany. Sylvia is an internationally well known authoresse on the topic on „Nanomaterials in Architecture, Interior Architecture and Design" (Birkhauser Publ.) and recently edited the internationally fundamental book on interiors „Designing Interior Architecture" (Birkhauser publ.). Her studio's work has been awarded several times. Furthermore she's vice president of BDIA (German Association of Interior Architects) and delegate for IFI (International Federation of Interior Architects/Designers).

Iris Mach holds a Ph.D in science and is a faculty of Architecture at the Vienna University of Technology (VUT), Austria. She researches and teaches in the fields "Disaster Mitigation" and "Applied Aesthetics" and is in charge of the scientific cooperation program between the VUT and Japanese universities. She graduated from the VUT and stayed at the University of Tokyo as a postgraduate research student in the framework of her doctoral studies on the topic of staged spaces in traditional and modern Japanese architecture, which she finished back in Vienna.

Gregory Marinic is Director of Interior Architecture and Assistant Professor at Gerald D. Hines College of Architecture, University of Houston. Gregory is director and co-founder of d3, a New York-based art/architecture/design stewardship organization and principal of Archipelago, a New York- and Houston-based architectural practice engaged in design, research, teaching, and experimentation. He holds a Master of Architecture degree from the University of Maryland and a Bachelor of Science degree in Geography/Urban Planning from

Ohio University. Gregory currently serves as editor of *AIA Forward Journal, International Journal of the Arts in Society, Design Principles and Practices*, IDEC Exchange, and *d3:dialog*. His recent publications include *Design Issues, International Journal of Architectural Research, Design Principles and Practices, International Journal of the Arts in Society*, and various publications of Seoul-based Damdi Architecture Publishing Ltd. and the Association of Collegiate Schools of Architecture.

Lore Mellemans studied Interior Architecture at the PHL University College in Belgium and finished her master year in reuse of buildings in 2013. During this master year she went on an Erasmus exchange to Milan, Italy. Her interest in industrial heritage led her to writing a masters thesis on the reuse of cooling towers.

Bie Plevoets studied Interior Architecture at the PHL University College (Belgium) and followed a postgraduate master in Conservation of Monuments and Sites at the Raymond Lemaire International Centre for Conservation (KU Leuven). Since 2010 Bie Plevoets is working on a Ph.D research at Hasselt University in which she explores the position of adaptive reuse whitin the discipline of interior architecture, with specific focus on projects with retail as a new function. Beside research, she teaches several courses on adaptive reuse in the bachelor and master Interior Architecture at Hasselt University.

Pari Riahi is a part-time faculty at Rhode Island School of Design, where she has been teaching for the past 6 years in multiple capacities in the architecture and INTAR (interior architecture and adaptive reuse) departments and a principal of her architectural office in Western Massachusetts. Pari completed her PhD dissertation under the supervision of Prof. Alberto Perez-Gomez at McGill University in 2010. Her thesis, "Ars et Ingenium: The Embodiment of Imagination in Architectural Drawings of the Quattrocento," concerns the reciprocity of architectural drawings and imagination in the work of Francesco di Giorgio Martini and will be published by Routledge in 2014. Pari's current research interests track the propagation of digital media and the effect of new technologies on architectural thinking and practice. Concurrently she is working on a study of subsidized housing and territorial conditions of the underprivileged suburbs of Paris. Pari has previously taught at MIT and SUNY Buffalo and has participated in many conferences and symposia.

Susan Rogers is an Assistant Professor of Architecture at the University of Houston and the Director of the Community Design Resource Center (CDRC). Her research, teaching, and practice focus on design as a strategy for community change, exploring the seams between design, justice and the public interest.

Jorg Sieweke is a licensed urban designer and landscape architect from Berlin. He has taught in Berlin, Stuttgart and Dresden and currently teachers at RWTH Aachen University in Germany. Since 2009 he has served as an Assistant Professor in Landscape Architecture at the University of Virginia, where he directs a design/research initiative "ParadoXcity" focusing on re-envisioning civic infrastructure in Venice, New Orleans and Baltimore. Sieweke recently chaired the 2013 International "Woltz Symposium" titled "QuasiObject / HyperObject / WorldObjects" at the University of Virginia and received the CELA 2013 Excellence in Design Studio Teaching Award.

Marco Vanucci is the director and founder of OPEN-SYSTEMS Architecture, an emerging architectural and design practice currently working on mid to large-scale projects in Europe and North Africa. He worked for Zaha Hadid Architects and AKTII Part Team where he developed his interest for organizational and performative systems and the middle ground between architecture and engineering. He has lectured internationally and his work has been part of several international exhibitions in Europe and North America. He has taught at KTH in Stockholm and he currently teaches at the Architectural Association Diploma School in London.

Emily Yeung is a UK qualified Architect practicing in London. She graduated from the Bartlett School of Architecture with Distinction, where she was included in the Dean's list for Outstanding design achievements. Born in HK and raised in Canada, she went on to complete her undergraduate degree in England at the University of Cambridge. Emily is interested in the cultural typology of the city and how it manifests itself between architecture and technology. Her design work has featured in galleries and has won numerous awards, with her work exhibited and presented for the opening of AIA Architecture week 2011 and London Design 2012 Exhibition at Dreamspace gallery.

EDITORS

Ernesto Aparicio is a Senior Critic in the Graphic Design Department at RISD. He earned his BA at the Escuela de Bellas Artes, La Plata, Buenos Aires and did his Post Graduate Studies at the Ecole des Art Decoratifs, Paris. Prior to moving to the US he served as Art Director for Editions du Seuil in Paris, while maintaining his own Graphic Design practice, Aparicio Design Inc. Best known for his work in the world of publishing, his work has also included corporate identities, publications and way-finding for corporations and institutions in France, Japan, and the US. He has recently been named Creative Director for the New York design firm, DFA.

Markus Berger is an Associate Professor and Graduate Program Director in the Department of Interior Architecture at RISD. He holds an Diplomingenieur für Architektur from the Technische Universität Wien, Austria and is a registered architect (SBA) in the Netherlands. Prior to coming to the US he practiced as an architect and taught in Austria, India, Pakistan and with UN Studio in the Netherlands. He currently heads his own design studio in Providence, InsideOut Interventions focusing on design interventions and research such as forms of *CHANGE* in the built environment and *UMBAU*, design interventions that take sensory experience as an essential part of the whole. He is a co-founder and co-editor of the Int|AR Journal.

Damian F. White is Head of the Department of History, Philosophy and the Social Sciences, Associate Professor of Sociology and Coordinator of Nature-Culture-Sustainability Studies at the Rhode Island School of Design. He is the author of *Bookchin: A Critical Appraisal (Pluto Press, 2008); The Environment, Nature and Social Theory: Critical Hybridities* (Macmillian, 2015); and co-editor with Chris Wilbert of *Technonatures* (Wilfred Laurier Press, 2009) and *Autonomy, Solidarity, Possibility: The Colin Ward Reader* (AK Press, 2011).

Liliane Wong is Professor and Head of the Department of Interior Architecture at RISD. She received her MArch from Harvard University, Graduate School of Design and a B.A. in Mathematics from Vassar College. She is a registered Architect in Massachusetts and has practiced in the Boston area including in her firm, MWA where she focused on the design of libraries. She is a co-designer of the library furniture system, Kore. A long time volunteer at soup kitchens, her teaching emphasizes the importance of public engagement in architecture and design. She is a co-founder and co-editor of the Int|AR Journal.